CREATIVITY

What
Is
It?

Daniel
Cohen

M. Evans and Company, Inc.   New York, New York 10017

M. Evans and Company titles are distributed in
the United States by the J. B. Lippincott Company,
East Washington Square, Philadelphia, Pa. 19105;
and in Canada by McClelland & Stewart Ltd.,
25 Hollinger Road, Toronto M4B 3G2, Ontario

Library of Congress Cataloging in Publication Data

Cohen, Daniel.
    Creativity, what is it?

    Bibliography: p.
    Includes index.
    SUMMARY: Considers what creativity is, how it is
measured, what influences it, and the relationship
between creativity and brain waves and dreaming.
    1. Creative ability—Juvenile literature.
[1. Creative ability] I. Title.
BF408.C58 1977   153.3′5   77-23481
ISBN 0-87131-245-X

The quotations from Bonnie Cashin, George Nelson,
and Noam Chomsky that appear in Chapter 3 are reprinted
from *The Creative Experience* by Stanley Rosner and
Lawrence E. Abt. Copyright © 1970 by Stanley Rosner
and Lawrence E. Abt.
Reprinted by permission of Grossman Publishers.

The creativity tests that appear on page 74
are reprinted from *Creativity and Intelligence:
Explorations with Gifted Students*
by Jacob Getzels and Philip Jackson.
Copyright © 1962 by Jacob Getzels and Philip Jackson.

Manufactured in the United States of America

9 8 7 6 5 4 3 2 1

To Roz and Steve Shaw

Contents

CREATIVITY

1

What is Creativity?

Today everybody wants to be creative. You can take courses in creative writing, creative painting, creative pottery-making, and creative woodworking. Books have been written on the subject of creative cooking, creative sewing, creative childraising, creative education, creative marriage and divorce, even creative aggression. I have not run across a book on creative destruction, but I would not be surprised if one exists. A state of creative tension is supposed to be highly beneficial.

If creative is not the most overworked word in the English language, it must be near the top of the list. It has been used so many times, in so many different ways that it has practically lost its meaning altogether. Often creative is simply a popular synonym for "good" or "correct."

In spite of its overuse, the word does actually have a meaning, though not a scientifically precise one. A dictionary definition of creativity is the ability to make or produce something new and unique.

Within so broad a definition there is a lot of room for

argument. What exactly is new or unique? Must that which is created be useful? One could argue endlessly. Like so many abstract concepts, creativity is one of those things that we cannot define precisely but generally know when we see it.

Mankind has always considered creativity important. The very first words of the Bible are "In the beginning God created the heaven and the earth."

For much of human history, creativity has been regarded as a God-like attribute. Among the ancient Egyptians, the man who designed the first pyramid was later worshiped as a god.

Pythagoras was the ancient Greek philosopher who laid the foundations for much of modern mathematics and astronomy. He first proposed the idea that the world was round some two thousand years before Christopher Columbus demonstrated that concept. Pythagoras also founded a secret religious sect. He installed himself as not only the leader but the divine leader. He always spoke to his disciples through a curtain in order to heighten the godlike effect.

When the creative person himself was not actually regarded as divine, then the act of creation was invested with divine or at least mysterious and unfathomable qualities. The creative idea struck unexpectedly, like lightning. And with nearly as much force.

Probably the most famous single story about creativity concerns the ancient Greek mathematician and engineer Archimedes. Hiero, the tyrant of Syracuse, had just received a new golden crown, but he suspected that the goldsmith had adulterated the precious metal. So he asked Archimedes, to whom he was related, to find out whether his crown was pure gold, but without damaging it in any way.

Archimedes knew that all metals were lighter than gold. He could weigh the crown and compare that weight with an equal amount of gold. If the weights were the same the crown was pure gold. If the crown weighed less then it had been adulterated. But how was he to determine the volume of the crown so that he would know how much gold to compare it with?

That problem stopped him. Then one day as he was stepping into his bath, as he had done hundreds of times before, he noticed that the water level rose and the tub overflowed. Here was the solution to his problem. In a flash he realized that the volume of water that was displaced was equal to the volume of the portion of the body he inserted into the water. He could dip the crown in water and find its volume by measuring the rise in the level of the water.

Archimedes was so elated by his discovery that, according to the story, he jumped out of his bath and ran through the streets of Syracuse stark naked shouting "Eureka! Eureka!," which is Greek for "I've got it! I've got it!" Ever since then the word eureka has often been used to announce an important and sudden discovery.

The end of the story, by the way, is that the crown had been adulterated with silver and the goldsmith was executed.

For the Greeks and many others creativity seemed an exceedingly rare quality, the sole property of a genius like Archimedes and not something that could be shared by the common run of mankind.

Throughout the middle ages it was assumed that all

creative inspiration was due to the direct intervention of God. Individual genius meant nothing. It was all the result of His will. Indeed, innovation was often discouraged because of the fear that it broke the traditional order established by the Church, and that its origin might be diabolical. Galileo, one of the great creative geniuses of all time, was threatened with torture unless he recanted some of his ideas about astronomy and the position the earth holds in the universe.

Often creativity was assumed to be the property of a small class of "geniuses" who were touched by a divine spark. Less charitably it was called a byproduct of madness. It has only been within the last fifty years or so that creativity has been regarded as a quality that is widespread in the human species. In addition to being widespread, it is also considered a quality that is highly desirable, and something that can be, at least to a degree, developed.

An enormous amount has been written about creativity. There have been books by poets and philosophers, psychiatrists and educators, and many others. A small and general introductory book such as this one cannot hope to survey the field. Much of the writing about creativity has been highly theoretical, personal, and subjective. While such work may be of great interest, and quite possibly of great significance, much of it really can't be tested or verified in a scientific manner.

What I have tried to do in this book is concentrate on those aspects of creativity that can be tested or examined objectively. I have adopted a very left-brained approach. What I mean by that will be explained in a later chapter. I haven't been able to stick to this approach completely. In some chapters I have had to rely, and rely heavily, on personal testimonies and on theories that are beyond our ability to test. Still, whenever possible, I have leaned toward the concrete and the measurable.

This is a bias, I admit. I started out with the premise that creativity is not some force from above but a product of the human brain. As such, it should be understandable. We should be able to figure out how it works and why. Perhaps we haven't succeeded very well yet, but the effort is worthwhile.

Not everyone agrees with that point of view. Many feel that current efforts to measure and understand creativity as a function of the brain are ludicrously inadequate and probably useless and misleading. There are many more who think that creativity is in fact mysterious and beyond our powers of understanding. But if these points of view are correct, it seems to me that there is very little to be gained in discussing the subject at all.

In any event, you should take into account the bias with which this book is written.

In keeping with that bias we are going to start our inquiry about as far from the idea of the "divine spark" of creativity as one can get. We are not even going to start with human beings. We are going to start with apes.

2

The Creative Ape

There is a picture hanging in my office that most visitors do not comment on. It is a thick semicircular smear of tempera paint, half blue and half red. Crude brush strokes stick out from the main body of the smear. To tell the truth, it is not a very attractive picture, but it is nicely framed and hangs in a prominent spot.

That is the reason that most people do not comment on it. People think I like it, and they don't want to insult me by telling me it looks awful. If I press them for an opinion I get comments like "interesting" or "it has a certain boldness." Perhaps some people even think that they *should* like it and are missing something because they don't. They fear that if they express their real opinion, that the picture is an ugly smear, they will reveal their artistic ignorance.

In fact, I wouldn't care what people say. The picture was painted by a gorilla at the Bronx Zoo. It was given to

16

me as a birthday present by my wife who has a sense of humor about such things.

The mere existence of "ape art" absolutely infuriates many painters. They say that paintings made by gorillas, chimpanzees, and the like are not "art" at all but merely random blotches of color. They also say that ape art is often used to ridicule modern art.

Ape pictures have been submitted to art contests without the judges' being told of the origin of the painting. So have framed paint rags and paintings created by a brush attached to the tail of a horse. In some cases these oddities have actually picked up prizes and given anti-modern art people a good laugh. Small wonder that ape art is deeply resented in some quarters.

It is easy enough to tell the difference between a painting by an ape and one by Rembrandt, Norman Rockwell, or even a six-year-old child. It is not always easy for the untrained eye (my untrained eye anyway) to tell the difference between a painting produced by an ape and those produced by the leading exponents of certain schools of abstract art.

But good or bad, is the ape art really art? Are animals capable of creative behavior?

Since we have never been able to adequately define creativity, there are obvious difficulties in answering such a question, but we can at least approach it.

At one time it was popularly believed that animals acted from "instinct" alone: that is, that their responses to every situation were determined by certain inborn behavior patterns. We now know that this view is incorrect. Animals, particularly those high on the evolutionary scale, do learn and can adapt their behavior to changing

*A young orangutan at the Bronx Zoo
with one of his paintings.*

situations. Moreover, tests have shown that they display a higher degree of what we would call intelligence than had previously been suspected.

But what about creativity? Do animals possess the ability to innovate, to make something new? We do know that a large number of animal species use natural objects in order to attain some goal, usually food. The woodpecker finch probes for beetles under the bark of a tree with a long thorn he holds in his beak. The sea otter cracks open shellfish on a flat stone that he places on his stomach. But such behavior patterns seem to be inborn. The finches and the otters do not "invent" these "tools" anew every generation.

It is only when we get to man's closest relations, the apes, that questions about creativity begin to have any meaning. Over the last fifteen years there has been much talk of the intelligence of such large sea mammals as whales and dolphins. While there is little doubt that these creatures do stand high in any ranking of intelligent animals, most biologists think that accounts of their intelligence have been exaggerated. In any event, we know relatively little about their behavior in the wild. Attempts to test them in captivity have been limited. Dolphins are adapted to an entirely different environment. They live in water, they get most of their information through sound not sight, and they do not possess hands with which to manipulate objects. We simply do not have adequate tests for such animals. Besides, most whales are just too big to keep in captivity.

The apes, however, have been extensively tested, with intriguing results. The earliest experiments were carried on in the years before World War II by the German scientist Wolfgang Kohler. Kohler chose chimpanzees as his subjects for a series of classic experiments. The chimpanzee is generally considered the most advanced of the apes.

In one experiment, tempting food was placed just out of reach of a caged chimp. The chimp was also given a stick. In the wild chimpanzees normally use sticks for poking and hitting. The chimp would first poke at the food with his stick, then hit at it. But very soon the chimp discovered that the only way to get the food was to manipulate the stick in a raking motion. After once making this "discovery," the chimps were regularly able to rake in the food outside of their cage. They had solved the problem.

The next test was much more difficult. This time the chimp was given two sticks. neither one of which was long enough to reach the food. But the sticks were of hollow bamboo. One could be fitted inside the other to make a stick long enough to reach the food. Most of Kohler's chimps could never figure this out; but one named Sultan did master the trick, though not without some difficulty.

Kohler observed Sultan's ineffectual attempts to pull in the food with a too short stick. He even gave Sultan a hint by putting one finger into the opening at the end of the larger stick, although without pointing to the other stick. This had no effect on Sultan. After about an hour Sultan seemed to get discouraged, and Kohler went on to other tasks leaving the ape in care of a keeper. Then something happened, as the keeper reported:

> Sultan first of all squats indifferently on the box, which has been left standing a little back from the railings; then

he gets up, picks up the two sticks, sits down again on the box and plays carelessly with them. While doing this, it happens that he finds himself holding one rod in either hand in such a way that they lie in a straight line; he pushes the thinner one a little way into the opening of the thicker, jumps up and is already on the run towards the railings, to which he has now half turned his back, and begins to draw a banana towards him with the double stick. I call [Kohler]; meanwhile, one of the animal's rods has fallen out of the other, as he has pushed one of them only a little way into the other; whereupon he connects them again.

From then on Sultan never had any difficulty connecting two rods and later even three.

Later still, Sultan learned how to bite splinters off a large stick so that it could be made thinner and fit into a hollow stick.

Had Sultan known Greek, Kohler commented, he would certainly have shouted "Eureka!" Sultan, Kohler observed, was a genius among chimps. Many of the other animals could not master the task at all.

The apes tested by Russian researcher Nadie Kohts made a different kind of tool. She gave her chimps a metal pipe with food crammed inside out of reach. The chimps were then given a board and would tear splinters off it with their teeth or hands. They would poke the splinters inside of the tube in order to dislodge the food.

In the wild, chimpanzees display much the same behavior. Jane Goodall, who pioneered the study of the behavior of wild chimpanzees, found that they would strip the leaves off a twig and poke the twig into a termite mound in order to get termites, which they love to eat. The chimps took a natural object, a twig, and altered it for a purpose. This fulfilled the definition of tool-making behavior.

The experiments with chimpanzees in captivity had always been a bit suspect anyway. The apes were, after all, not operating under "natural" conditions. Goodall's observation proved to be a sensation. Here wild apes, without any aid from their human captors, were "creating" a tool. That was something that only human beings were supposed to be able to do.

Persuading apes to make drawings and paintings had a more serious purpose than simply to irritate abstract artists. The zoologist Desmond Morris, who conducted extensive tests at the London Zoo, found that young chimpanzees loved to paint. They would do it repeatedly without any special training or reward. "The activity is entirely self-rewarding—it is, if you like, an art for art's sake," wrote Morris in the book *Men and Apes*.

Morris's champion artist was a young male chimp named Congo. During a three-year period of testing, Congo produced 384 drawings and paintings. He was able to work at his art for about half an hour at a stretch. After that he got bored. He also didn't like to work more than a few sessions each week.

But Congo needed no encouragement to start his art work. All he was ever shown was how to hold a pencil. No one guided his hand or showed him how to make different strokes. All of Congo's art came out of his own graphic explorations.

There was a distinct progression in Congo's work. His style changed from month to month. Morris notes in *Men and Apes*:

Small jerky lines gave way to broad sweeping curves, until eventually he was making reasonably accurate circles. His highest peak of development came with the construction of a circle which was then marked inside. It is particularly tantalizing that in human infant picture making this stage is the vital precursor to the very first pictorial representation—that of the face. As soon as the child sees that marks inside the circle look vaguely like features, it begins to organize them into eyes, mouth and nose. From this point on, it leaves abstract scribbles behind and plunges into the exciting new world of representation. Unhappily this is the point at which the apes get stuck. No infra-human creature has yet been able to make a recognisable representation of any kind. Exactly why it fails, we cannot say. It struggles right to the very threshold and then halts.

Morris hopes that one day a "super chimp" will be found who will be able to go beyond the limits reached by Congo and other apes. Morris believes there is a "faint chance" that such an animal may be discovered. But so far success has been elusive. He also laments that research in such areas is extremely limited.

One criticism of the ape art is that the apes are not really making pictures at all but simply engaging in a form of "arm gymnastics"—that is, pushing a brush or pencil across paper with no reference at all to what the results look like. Ape art, say some critics, is no more art than hen scratchings in sand.

Morris and his associates gave Congo a series of test papers with different geometric shapes and lines already on them. When given one of these special papers instead of a blank sheet, Congo promptly reorganized his customary drawing pattern. If he was given a paper with a square in the middle he tended to concentrate his marks in that square. If the square was placed on one side of the paper Congo generally tried to balance it by making his marks on the other side of the paper. A square at the top seemed to encourage Congo to concentrate his marks at the bottom of the paper. Morris believes that Congo possessed a "basic sense of graphic composition, crude admittedly, but nevertheless distinct."

A gorilla named Sophie at the Rotterdam Zoo produced similar results with test papers.

Since these early experiments, ape art has become less of a novelty, though the exploration of its possible significance has not progressed very far. The Bronx Zoo regularly sells gorilla paintings like the one that I have. It is a money-making scheme, for the zoo, like so many worthy public institutions, is hard-pressed for funds today. Congo's pictures look better than the gorilla picture I have.

But is it art? Can chimpanzees really "create" tools in the wild or in captivity? The answers to such questions depend on one's definition of creativity. For myself I am satisfied that the apes have taken the first halting step on the road to creativity.

Not so very long ago such an opinion would have seemed absurd, even shocking, for, as we shall see, creativity had been endowed with mystic, nearly divine qualities.

3

The Creative Experience

In answering the question, How are poems made? my instinctive answer is a flat "I don't know." It makes not the slightest difference that the question as asked me refers solely to my own poems, for I know as little of how they are made as I do of any one else's. What I do know about them is only a millionth part of what there must be to know. I meet them where they touch consciousness, and that is already a considerable distance along the road to evolution.

So wrote the American poet Amy Lowell. She continued, "A common phrase among poets is, 'it came to me.' So hackneyed has this become that one learns to suppress the expression with care, but really it is the best description I know of the conscious arrival of a poem."

Amy Lowell's puzzlement about how she did her work is not unique among creative people. When asked to describe how they did this or that, even those who are masters of language often stumble and become nearly

Amy Lowell: "How are poems made? I don't know."

incoherent. Scientists who deal in precise and logical details can come out sounding like poets, or even mystics. They too are often forced to fall back on the trite "it came to me," or something similar.

Some creative people don't like to talk about the process at all. They may feel that discussion is useless, or they may fear that talking about creativity will somehow damage the delicate process.

"It is a mistake for the sculptor or a painter to speak or write very often about his job," wrote the sculptor Henry Moore. "It releases tension needed for his work. By trying to express his aims with rounded-off logical exactness, he can easily become a theorist whose actual work is only a caged-in exposition of conceptions evolved in terms of logic and words."

But despite their reservations and uncertainties and downright puzzlement, artists, musicians, scientists, and other creative people have written and spoken about the creative experience. In this chapter we will look at some of the things that they have said, with particular emphasis on the question of where a creative person gets his or her ideas.

Probably the best-known piece of "writing on writing" is Edgar Allan Poe's *The Philosophy of Composition*. It is also one of the oddest—odd in that it is so matter of fact.

Poe is the acknowledged master of the macabre. His stories and poems are filled with ghastly and nightmarish images. His writings abound with references to dreams, visions, and strong, overpowering emotions. Poe's own life was scarcely less of a horror story than some of his fictional creations. He was dogged by poverty, illness, and personal tragedy. Aside from his bad luck, he was considered distinctly strange; for example, he married a thirteen-year-old girl, and he was an alcoholic. Indeed, it was his drinking that finally killed him.

If ever there was an individual who appeared destined to dash off tales and poems in some sort of feverish trance, it was Edgar Allan Poe. Yet when he sat down to describe the creation of his celebrated poem "The Raven," he made it sound anything but feverish and trancelike. Poe explained how the subject matter, the meter, even the very words of the poem were chosen by a process of conscious deliberation.

He wanted to write a melancholy poem. What subject could be more melancholy, Poe asks, than the death of a beautiful woman?

> From my books surcease of sorrow—sorrow for the lost Lenore—For that rare and radiant maiden whom the angels named Lenore—
>
> Nameless here for evermore.

The raven, a well-known symbol of death, was naturally picked for that reason. Even the raven's repeated phrase "Nevermore" was chosen, said Poe, for its "sonorous" or gravely imposing quality.

According to Poe's own testimony, the poem "The Raven" was manufactured much as one might imagine a computer, if properly programmed, would turn out a "melancholy" poem.

Poe's essay offends a lot of people, particularly those who like to find the creative process something divine and mysterious. One response is to say that "The Raven" is not a very good poem. But Poe indicates that he wrote

Poe's Raven: Inspiration or conscious deliberation?

other works in the same calculating way, and there are undoubted masterpieces among his short stories.

Another way of refuting Poe is to say that he was simply not telling the truth. I first read Poe's essay in high school. It was included in a collection of American writing that was required reading. After reading the essay I vividly recall our English teacher's telling the class that Poe was a liar because poems were not and could not be composed in the manner that he described. This incident has stuck in my mind because it was the only time any of my high school teachers flatly contradicted something that appeared in a book of required readings. My high school English teacher isn't the only one to have held a low opinion of Poe's essay. The poet Brewster Ghiselin, who edited a collection of writings on creativity called *The Creative Process*, says of Poe that he was "possibly insincere."

One reason that Poe's description of the creative process may seem so surprising is that we have a limited view of him. His horror fiction and disorderly personal life are only part of the picture. He was also an editor, a professional writer, and a perceptive literary critic.

He did not necessarily write in order to satisfy some obscure creative urge; he wrote because that is how he made his living. He had deadlines to meet, and stories and poems he turned out fetched the money to pay the bills (often there was not enough money). As a critic he was able to dissect the writings of others with the same cold thoroughness that he used on "The Raven."

While Poe's description of the creative process may be the most mechanical on record, he is not the only one to have taken an unromantic attitude. The Russian short-story writer Anton Chekhov said: ". . . to deny that artistic creation, involves problems and purposes would be to admit that an artist creates without premeditation, without design, under a spell. Therefore if an artist boasted to me of having written a story without a previously settled design, but by inspiration, I should call him a lunatic."

The eighteenth-century writer Samuel Johnson put the matter even more unromantically: "No man but a blockhead ever wrote, except for money."

Inventor Thomas Alva Edison once quipped that his work was 1 percent inspiration and 99 percent perspiration.

The testimony of such eminent and creative individuals certainly cannot be laid aside. But such opinions are in the minority. Many more creative people in all fields would probably subscribe to Amy Lowell's dictum, "it just came to me." There is a wealth of evidence that the creative process is at least a little mysterious to most of those who do the creating.

More typical is this description by the American novelist Thomas Wolfe (quoted in Ghiselin's collection *The Creative Process*) of how some of his books were written.

> It was a process that began in a whirling vortex and a creative chaos and that proceeded slowly at the expense of infinite confusion, toil and error toward clarification and the articulation of an ordered and formal structure. . . .
>
> I cannot really say the book was written. It was something that took hold of me and possessed me, and before I was done with it—that is, before I finally emerged with the first completed part—it seemed to me that it had been done for me. It was exactly as if this great black storm cloud I have spoken of had opened up and, mid flashes of light-

ning, was pouring from its depth a torrential and ungovernable flood. Upon that flood everything was swept and borne along as by a great river. And I was borne along with it.

The British poet A. E. Housman finds the creative process somewhat less violent. He uses the metaphor of a bubbling spring instead of a thunderstorm or a rushing river. But still, the experience he describes has many basic similarities to what Thomas Wolfe described.

Having drunk a pint of beer at luncheon—beer is a sedative to the brain, and my afternoons are the least intellectual portion of my life—I would go out for a walk of two or three hours. As I went along, thinking of nothing in particular, only looking at things around me and following the progress of the seasons, there would flow into my mind, with sudden and unaccountable emotion, sometimes a line or two of verse, sometimes a whole stanza at once, accompanied, not preceded, by a vague notion of the poem which they were destined to form part of. Then there would usually be a lull of an hour or so, then perhaps the spring would bubble up again. I say bubble up, because, so far as I could make out, the source of the suggestions thus proffered to the brain was an abyss, . . . the pit of the stomach.

The testimony of the American novelist Dorothy Canfield (as quoted in Ghiselin's book, *The Creative Process*) also contains some of the same themes.

Everybody knows such occasional hours or days of freshened emotional responses when events that usually pass almost unnoticed, suddenly move you deeply, when a sunset lifts you to exaltation, when a squeaking door throws you into a fit of exasperation, when a clear look of trust in a child's eyes moves you to tears, or an injustice reported in the newspapers to flaming indignation, a good action to a sunny warm love of human nature, a discovered meanness in yourself or another to despair.

I have no idea whence this tide comes, or where it goes, but when it begins to rise in my heart, I know that a story is hovering in the offing.

Writers, of course, are not the only creative people who have such impulses or inspirations (though they seem to write about them most frequently, probably because of the nature of their profession). In practically every field of creative endeavor there are those who have described almost identical experiences and feelings.

In a letter attributed to Mozart, the composer explains how he got some of his musical ideas.

When I am, as it were, completely myself, entirely alone, and of good cheer—say, travelling in a carriage, or walking after a good meal, or during the night when I cannot sleep; it is on such occasions that my ideas flow best and most abundantly. Whence and how they come, I know not; nor can I force them. Those ideas that please me I retain in memory, and am accustomed, as I have been told, to hum them to myself. If I continue in this way, it soon occurs to me how I may turn this or that morsel to account, so as to make a good dish of it, that is to say, agreeably to the rules of counterpoint, to the peculiarities of the various instruments, etc. All this fires my soul, and, provided I am not disturbed, my subject enlarges itself, becomes methodised and defined, and the whole, though it be long, stands almost complete and finished in my mind, so that I can survey it, like a fine picture or a beautiful statue, at a glance. . . .

The contemporary fashion designer Bonnie Cashin was asked where her ideas came from. She replied:

This is hard to pinpoint. Actually my work, I guess, is always on my mind even when I'm looking at a marvelous sky or watching a play, or on holiday. I'm constantly re-designing subconsciously. I can only see in color. I look at everything in relationships. Ideas just pop into my mind out of the blue seemingly. I jot them down. . . .

Sometimes ideas tumble upon each other. This is ex-hilarating. Sometimes they just don't come. I can't even draw. At those times I'll try to quit. There's no use strug-gling. However, when I know I have a job to finish I just get to it. I think professionals get the habit of meeting deadlines.

Industrial design would seem to be a practical, hard-headed endeavor. Yet when industrial designer George Nelson was asked how he got his ideas, he had no practical or hard-headed answers to supply.

I think the factors must be pretty common to all people who do solve problems. I think that what is loosely called "creativity" is really a description of a problem-solving activity in one form or another, and where ideas come from is, I believe, rather mysterious, but I will try by hindsight at least to recapitulate some of the process. I would say that one of the main triggers is irritation. You look at a situation and suddenly see it with fresh eyes. Then the status quo, whatever it is, becomes very annoying and some kind of pressure builds up more or less unconsciously, and apparently one works away at this problem with a view to getting rid of the irritation. At some point, if one is lucky, the thing explodes.

The linguist Noam Chomsky actually dreams about the problems he must solve. While being interviewed for the book *Explorations in Creativity*, Chomsky was asked:

Q: Would it be fair to say, then, that you have the problems you're working on in the back of your mind all the time?

A: All the time, yes, I dream about them. But I wouldn't call dreaming very different from really working.

Q: Do you literally mean dreaming?

A: Yes, I mean it literally. Examples and problems are sort of floating through my mind very often at night. Sometimes, when I am sleeping fitfully, the problems that I've been working on are often passing through my mind.

Q: Do they pass through your mind in a dream in the same form in which you were working on them?

A: Well, as far as I know, in exactly the same form. The dream life doesn't seem to have a different framework or to involve a different approach. So it's just a sort of slightly less concentrated and conscious version of the same thing during the day.

The great nineteenth-century German scientist Hermann Ludwig Ferdinand Von Helmholtz discussed the problem of creativity at a banquet in honor of his seventieth birthday. He said that after examining a problem

... in all directions, ... happy ideas come unexpectedly without effort, like an inspiration. So far as I am concerned, they have never come to me when my mind was fatigued, or when I was at my working table. . . . They came particularly readily during the slow ascent of wooded hills on a sunny day.

Helmholtz divided the process of creation into three distinct parts. The first he called "preparation," the time when all the important information was collected and organized. The second was "incubation," the time when one was not consciously thinking about the problem. The third stage was when the "happy idea" suddenly surfaced. After that there followed a great deal of hard work in which the "happy idea" was verified.

Jules Henri Poincaré, a brilliant French mathematician of the late nineteenth and early twentieth century, left one of the fullest personal accounts of the creative process. He describes how he had been working on a difficult mathematical problem.

Just at this time I left Caen, where I was then living, to go on a geologic excursion under the auspices of the school of mines. The changes of travel made me forget my mathematical work. Having reached Coutances, we entered an omnibus to go some place or other. At the moment when I put my foot on the step the idea came to me, without anything in my former thoughts seeming to have paved the way for it, . . . I did not verify the idea; I should not have had time, as, upon taking my seat in the omnibus, I went on with a conversation already commenced, but I felt a perfect certainty. On my return to Caen, for conscience's sake, I verified the result at my leisure.

Then I turned my attention to the study of some arithmetical questions apparently without much success and without a suspicion of any connection with my preceding researches. Disgusted with my failure, I went to spend a few days at the seaside, and thought of something else. One morning, walking on the bluff, the idea came to me, with just the same characteristics of brevity, suddenness and immediate certainty. . . .

Unlike Poincaré, who recalled finishing his work without difficulty, most creative people report having to follow the initial inspiration with a great deal of hard work to complete the final product, book, picture, scientific discovery, or whatever. But the phenomenon of inspiration is a common one.

It is also a seductively attractive one, and the hard work is occasionally forgotten. There are any number of novels, epic poems, and books of philosophy which were supposedly written entirely by "inspiration." In most cases the writer claims that he sat down, without the faintest notion of what he was going to write. Then he was struck by some mysterious force, often called "inspiration." He wrote along furiously, without attention to style or anything else, until the work was finished. Many of these "automatic writers" say they had no idea of what they had written until it was finished.

Anyone who thinks that this method succeeds should be condemned to read some "inspired" novels or philosophical works produced from beginning to end by automatic writing. They are, most often, boring and repetitious, if not entirely incoherent.

Psychologists Stanley Rosner and Lawrence E. Abt edited the book of interviews with creative people called

The Creative Experience. In their conclusion they state:

> In science, mathematics and the arts, there is widespread
> recognition of the significant place occupied by intuition,
> unconscious promptings and inexplicable insights, and the
> sudden awareness of relationships. Scientific discovery
> and artistic creations are hardly the result solely of rational
> considerations. The repeated references in our own inter-
> views to "I don't know where the idea came from," and "It
> just came to mind," attest to functions in operation beyond
> the level of consciousness.

In this chapter we have stressed the nonrational side of
creativity. But a collection of subjective statements—as
interesting as they may be—are of limited value. If both
poets and industrial designers are often puzzled about
where they get their ideas, that tells us something, but
not much. We will now attempt some more concrete
examinations of the subject of creativity.

4

Creativity and Illness

Genius is next to madness, or at least so we have often been told. All artists are a little bit crazy, some more than a little bit, is another commonly held idea.

One might suspect that ideas of this type are supported by uncreative people in a sour grapes mood. "I'm no genius, but I'm not crazy either," they might say. Creative people often say and do disturbing things. Putting them down as crazy is an easy way of ignoring them.

Such motives undoubtedly have contributed to the eternal popularity of the genius-madness theory. But in fact, it has been held quite seriously by a great number of people. It comes up in virtually every discussion of creativity. It must be dealt with.

Another popular idea—though not as popular today as the madness theory—is that there is a relationship between physical illness and creativity. Poets in particular had a reputation for looking pale and sickly. That is a subject that can be gotten out of the way rather quickly.

During the nineteenth and early twentieth centuries,

tuberculosis, or consumption as it was usually called, was believed to be a positive aid to creativity. There was a theory that the low-grade fever induced by the infection somehow stimulated the mind.

A number of well-known artists did contract tuberculosis and died from it. Among the famous victims were the English poet John Keats, who died at the age of twenty-six in 1821, the Polish pianist and composer Frédéric Chopin, who died at the age of thirty-nine, and the author Robert Louis Stevenson, who died at the age of forty-four in 1894.

All three were rather dashing and romantic figures. These premature deaths from consumption contributed a great deal to the aura of artistic glamour that collected around the disease.

It was not uncommon in the nineteenth century for perfectly healthy young men who aspired to be poets to feign consumption. They would carry around handkerchiefs, into which they pretended to cough occasionally. They even smeared rouge on their cheeks to give themselves a properly flushed and feverish look.

In reality, there is nothing at all glamorous about tuberculosis. It is a terrible, wasting disease, and until the mid-twentieth century it was usually incurable and fatal.

The scientists René and Jean Dubois studied the history of the disease in their book *The White Plague: Tuberculosis, Man and Society*. They paid particular attention to any possible relationship between the disease and creativity. Their conclusion: "There is no evidence that tuberculosis breeds genius. The probability is, rather, that eagerness for achievement often leads to a way of life that renders the body less resistant to infection."

John Keats: An early death from consumption.

The British physician Sir George Pickering thinks that something else may be involved. In his book *Creative Malady* he points out: "The invalid with pulmonary tuberculosis used to be put to bed, and tended assiduously. Rest, good food, and protection from the more exacting affairs of life, were the established treatment."

The consumptive, if he was already gifted, might then have more opportunity to create just because he was an invalid. If properly cared for, he could live for years. It is also possible that because he knew that he had only a limited time to live, he may have been spurred on to greater efforts to get his work done while he could.

Still, pain, weakness, threat of an early death, and enforced confinement are rarely the best conditions for creativity. The great German novelist Thomas Mann spent time in a tuberculosis sanatorium. His novel *The Magic Mountain*, one of his finest works, draws on his experiences there. But the sanatorium merely provided the theme for his book. He produced good books both before and after his confinement for the disease.

Pickering says:

Organic or physical disease is not, to my knowledge, in general an aid to creativity. Vigour is essential to creativity. Many organic diseases are associated with pain, discomfort, fever and lack of energy. Many, too, give rise to fear, which tends to monopolise the mind and to displace productive activity.

Many studies of creative people have demonstrated that their physical health is as good or better than other people's. The pale, consumptive poet is more myth than a reality. Plenty of unpoetic people died young from tuberculosis.

But the problem of the relationship of creativity to mental illness is not so easily disposed of. While belief in a link between consumption and creativity may go back some two or three hundred years, the idea that creative genius is closely related to madness goes back at least to the ancient Greeks. The Greek philosopher Plato related inspiration to abnormality: "I have observed this about poets. It is not by taking thought that they create what they create; it is owing to a natural disposition and when ecstatically possessed." Plato's pupil Aristotle said that no great mind was free from a streak of madness. He did not, however, include his own.

According to Shakespeare:

> The lunatic, the lover and the poet
> Are of imagination all compact.

Shakespeare, who is generally accounted to be the greatest poet in the English language, should be granted a little poetic license for that statement. Though not much is known about Shakespeare's personal life, there is no hint that he was in any way a lunatic.

The nineteenth-century British essayist Charles Lamb strongly disagreed with Shakespeare. Lamb wrote:

So far from the position holding true, that great wit (or genius, in our modern way of speaking) has a necessary alliance with insanity, the greatest wits, on the contrary, will ever be found to be the sanest writers. It is impossible for the mind to conceive of a mad Shakespeare.

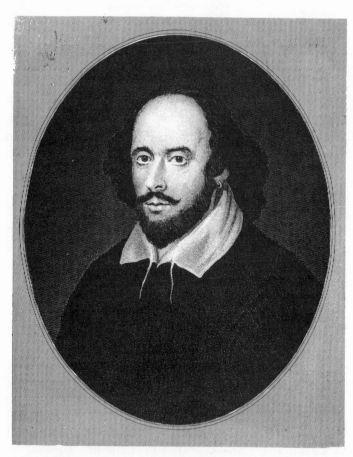

"*It is impossible for the mind to conceive*
of a mad Shakespeare."

Lamb knew something both about writing and madness. His own sister Mary Ann Lamb was the victim of one of the most curious cases of periodic insanity on record. During one of her fits she stabbed her invalid mother to death and gravely wounded her father. Yet during her sane periods she had loved both of them very dearly. To save his sister from the horrors of the nineteenth-century madhouse, Charles Lamb had himself declared her guardian. They lived together during Mary Ann's periods of sanity. She helped her brother with his work and was regarded as an intelligent and charming hostess by his many literary friends. When one of her periodic fits of insanity came upon her, she was bundled off to the madhouse where she was kept under restraints until the fit passed. This strange relationship went on for nearly forty years, until Charles Lamb's death.

Until recently, however, Charles Lamb's opinion on genius and madness may well have been in the minority. One of the difficulties in discussing the problem is a definition of madness. Madness is not a scientific term. The word insanity isn't much better. If you have ever followed the conflicting arguments of psychiatrists trying to decide whether a defendant on trial is or is not insane, you know that there is no agreed-upon definition of the word. Indeed there is no agreed-upon definition of the word "normal" either.

Generally psychiatrists divide mental illness into two broad categories. Severe mental illness is called psychosis; less severe mental illness is known as psychoneurosis, or simply neurosis in popular language. There is less argument about psychosis, for the symptoms are dramatic and obvious. There are times when the psychotic individual cannot function in the world at all. His behavior is often so bizarre that it immediately attracts attention, and the condition of the psychotic tends to deteriorate as time goes on. Deterioration isn't always present, however. Mary Ann Lamb was unquestionably psychotic, but there is no indication that her condition was any worse when she was seventy years old than when she was thirty. Some psychotic patients do appear to recover over time.

There were a number of creative geniuses who were undoubtedly psychotic. The painter Vincent Van Gogh spent much of his later life in mental institutions. Today he would probably be classed as a schizophrenic.

In 1959 psychiatrists E. Slater and A. Meyer did a study of the career of the nineteenth-century German composer Robert Schumann. At one time Schumann tried to drown himself in the Rhine river; he died in a mental institution. The psychiatrists concluded that Schumann was indeed psychotic. The cause of his illness may have been syphilis, which in its final stages often affects the brain.

The Swedish writer August Strindberg displayed distinct paranoid symptoms. He even wrote a book about his illness, which he considered an aid to his creativity. "Not everyone is capable of being mad; and, of those lucky enough to be capable of madness, not many have the courage for it."

There are many other creative geniuses who have been suspected of psychosis. The great Russian writer Feodor Dostoevsky and the German philosopher Friedrich Nietzsche are among those most frequently mentioned.

So it is reasonable to conclude that psychosis is no

absolute bar to creativity. But is the incidence of psychosis higher among creative people than among the general population? Does psychosis actually aid creativity as Strindberg maintained?

Harold Nicholson examined the lives of thirty-two famous British poets. Of this group, one, William Cowper, was a manic-depressive who attempted suicide on several occasions. Jonathan Swift always feared that he was going insane and ultimately did become quite senile. But this happened only after he was well into his seventies. None of the others could clearly be classed as psychotic on the basis of available information.

Nicholson found that this group of poets was by and large fairly healthy mentally and physically. It was his opinion that if the lives of thirty-two prominent lawyers or businessmen from the same period were examined, the percentages of mental and physical illness would be about the same as it was for the poets.

More recent studies of individuals who scored high on creativity tests or were rated as being highly creative by their fellow workers or supervisors, likewise turned up no evidence of an unusual degree of psychotic behavior.

Strindberg thought that his madness helped his creative output, and perhaps it did, but there is little evidence that it helped anyone else. Van Gogh had been turning out great paintings before the onset of his psychosis (though he had never been what could be called happy or well-balanced). There is no indication that his deteriorating mental condition improved his paintings. Schumann's work actually seemed to suffer; during periods when he was badly disturbed he turned out nothing at all.

Recently the American director Joshua Logan revealed

that for many years he had been a manic-depressive. This illness had been successfully treated with the chemical lithium. Logan is a great supporter of lithium therapy and clearly feels that his mental illness is in no way an aid to his creativity. Whatever success he had came in spite of the illness rather than because of it.

So the evidence from a variety of sources suggests that severe mental illness and creativity are not as Shakespeare said "all compact." Indeed, there seems to be no greater incidence of psychosis among the creative than among the noncreative.

Mystics, however, present a special problem. These are individuals who feel themselves directly in touch with God, or with some reality beyond the reach of ordinary senses. Today many mystics would probably be classified as psychotic for they often see things and hear voices. But mystics do not think of themselves as mad. In certain periods of history and in certain places a mystic can be a hero or a saint. Joan of Arc, who heard voices and saw angels, was both. Was she also psychotic? Many scholarly debates have been conducted on that subject. Each age seems to answer the question differently in conformity with the prevailing beliefs of the time.

William Blake, the nineteenth-century illustrator and poet, often went into trances and saw visions. He claimed that he was visited daily by a messenger from Heaven. An ordinary person who made such claims today might well be classed as psychotic. Yet Blake, who began to have his trances and visions quite early in life and continued having them until his death at the age of seventy, did not suffer any decline in mental condition. He was devoted to his wife, as she was to him. His friends found him gener-

Drawings by William Blake. The picture of the demon as a flea came to him in a vision.

ally agreeable and charming—though obviously rather strange.

During his lifetime he produced a great deal of work, under fairly difficult conditions. Blake often claimed that he translated his visions directly into drawings or poems. Blake's work is unique. Not everyone likes him, but no one doubts his originality. If there is such a thing as creative madness, then William Blake has to be accounted one of the prime examples. (Of course Blake was cracked, quipped author Edith Sitwell, but that was where the light shone through.)

A relationship between serious mental illness and creativity can be ruled out on the basis of present information. The single exception may be mystics—but that is a limited area of human experience, and one that is not well understood.

An examination of the relationship between creativity and psychoneurosis or less severe mental illness is much more difficult. The boundary between normal behavior and psychoneurotic behavior is far from clear. Different authorities give different definitions for both words. To help clarify the subject let's look at a few examples.

Samuel Johnson was considered, quite correctly, to be one of the greatest wits and most penetrating intellects of eighteenth-century England. The coffeehouses of eighteenth-century London were justly famous for their brilliant conversation—and Dr. Johnson was the brightest star.

But this brilliant and witty man was also subject to the deepest and blackest depressions. In his private papers he confided the fear that he was going to die and that his soul would be condemned to hell. Sometimes he was so overwhelmed by these feelings that he would go to his room, fall on his knees in prayer, and barely have the energy to rise again hours later.

So bleak were his moods that Johnson often felt that he was losing his mind. He instructed his housekeeper that if at any time madness seemed to overpower him, she should lock him in his room, place chains upon his legs, and even beat him if necessary. In the eighteenth century beating was a common "cure" for mental illness.

Johnson never did go mad. He died of dropsy at the age of seventy-five. His life was long and productive. In an age when most writers either had private incomes or patrons, Johnson managed to support himself solely by his own writings—no small accomplishment. No one who is able to take on life and to produce as Samuel Johnson did, can be considered psychotic. Yet he was certainly not "normal" either. But his strange obsessions did not appear to dry up his creative abilities. Did they help him in any way? Not as far as we can tell.

In *Creative Malady*, George Pickering makes much of the strange and possibly important case of Charles Darwin. Darwin had been an indifferent student who cared more about hunting than studies. But he had impressed some of his professors as a sturdy outdoorsman, with a passion for collecting specimens. So when the position of naturalist for the round-the-world trip of the H.M.S. *Beagle* came up, Darwin was recommended. He accepted the job with some reservations, for his father was strongly opposed.

The voyage of the H.M.S. *Beagle* lasted nearly five years, from December 27, 1831, to October 2, 1836.

Much of the time was spent in and around South America. The trip was not an easy one; long voyages in wooden sailing ships never were. The collecting trips that Darwin conducted ashore were arduous. He was often exposed to hardship and danger.

During this long and difficult period Darwin had his share of illnesses and was often seasick. But by and large the young naturalist seemed to be the healthiest member of the crew of the *Beagle*. Not only did he enjoy the voyage thoroughly, it was to be the turning point in his life. From Darwin's observations and collections grew his theory of evolution by natural selection. This was the single most significant idea in nineteenth-century biology, and one of the most significant in the entire history of science.

But it took over twenty years from the time that Darwin returned from his voyage until the publication of *The Origin of Species*, in which his views were fully explained and documented. Even then Darwin felt that he had been rushed into publication, because another naturalist named Alfred Russel Wallace had hit upon the same idea. Wallace sent an essay on the subject to Darwin, and the two agreed on joint publication of their ideas. Later Darwin expanded the brief paper into the massive book *The Origin of Species*. Whereas the original Wallace/Darwin paper had attracted little attention, Darwin's book kicked up a fuss, echoes of which can still be heard today.

Though they could easily have been rivals, Wallace and Darwin treated each other with unusual courtesy. Darwin offered Wallace the option of publishing his essay first. Wallace declined and later said that he had written his essay in three nights, while Darwin had labored for

Charles Darwin, the victim of a mysterious illness.

eighteen years. It was the mass of evidence that Darwin
had collected rather than the idea itself that was finally to
make the impact. That was what Darwin had assumed all
along.

But the Charles Darwin who published *The Origin of
Species* in 1859 was a vastly changed man from the vigorous young naturalist who had set out on the *Beagle*.
Within a few months after his return to England, Darwin
began to suffer from an illness; the symptoms grew pro-
gressively worse. For most of the period during which
The Origin of Species and his other scientific works were
composed, Darwin was an invalid and virtual recluse on
his country estate.

What was Darwin suffering from? No one knew then,
and no one is sure now. Darwin was a methodical man and
carefully recorded all of his symptoms. He thought that
he was afflicted with some sort of heart ailment. Pains in
the chest and general faintness and weakness seem to
have been his primary symptoms. He consulted a number
of physicians, but they could not come to any agreement.

When Darwin did die—at the age of seventy-three—it
was of a heart ailment. But the symptoms that he had
suffered throughout most of his life were very different
from those of his last two years. Heart failure is the most
common cause of death for men of his age. Most physicians do not believe that he had an ordinary heart ailment.
Indeed, when Darwin was in his sixties he began feeling
better, until the onset of the heart illness which finally
killed him.

A common theory is that during the voyage of the
Beagle Darwin contracted some sort of tropical disease.

In South America he was bitten by the *benchuca*, a large black bug which sometimes carries an infection called Chagas's disease. This infection often affects the heart after many years. However, Dr. A. W. Woodruff, a specialist in tropical diseases, writing in the *British Medical Journal*, insisted that Darwin's symptoms did not match those of Chagas's disease.

Some of the physicians that Darwin consulted in his own day were convinced that he was a hypochondriac. Hypochondria is no longer a popular term among medical men; it is regarded as just one of many manifestations of psychoneurosis. George Pickering and others who have studied Darwin's life believe that his long illness was a psychoneurosis rather than an organic illness.

Darwin was clearly not crazy in any sense of the term. Though his life was limited—he was not able to travel much, his social life was kept at a bare minimum, and any undue excitement caused him discomfort and sleepless nights—he was not really an unhappy man. His marriage was extremely happy; he had ten children, several of whom became very prominent. And of course there was his work. Though he could only work a few hours a day, his scientific output was prodigious, the result earthshaking. He made very good use of the time he had.

Even before he set out on the *Beagle* Darwin had some anxiety about the state of his heart. But he refused to consult a physician for fear that he would be told he could not go. During the voyage his heart never bothered him.

What triggered Darwin's psychoneurosis? Many theories have been offered. George Pickering's is the latest and, in terms of creativity, the most interesting.

When Darwin returned from his voyage, he had no theory of evolution. This occurred to him a few months later, after reading Thomas Malthus's essay *On Population*. (The same book inspired Wallace some eighteen years later.) But Darwin knew that his theory was just that, a theory, and that to amass proof for the theory would require an enormous amount of work. The voyage had made him a fairly prominent man. There were invitations to join scientific societies and to serve on committees. He had recently married, his family was wealthy, and social obligations pressed in on him.

Says Pickering, "Thus we need seek no further for the cause of Darwin's psychoneurosis. It was the conflict between his passionate desire to collect convincing evidence for his hypothesis and the threat imposed on his work by social intercourse."

In his autobiography Darwin observes: "Even illhealth, though it has annihilated several years of my life, has saved me from the distractions of society and amusement."

It certainly saved him from the controversy that greeted *The Origin of Species*. Others carried the banner of Darwinism into the meetings and lecture halls. Darwin stayed quietly on his country estate and continued his scientific work.

While illness may not have made Darwin creative, it allowed him time and serenity to use his creative genius.

Douglas Hubble, whose essay on Charles Darwin and psychotherapy is quoted by Pickering, wondered what might have happened if Darwin's illness had been correctly diagnosed and treated. Could Darwin's healthy vigor have been restored

without at the same time destroying the *Origin of Species*?
No one in his senses would attempt the perilous task.
. . . It is a terrifying thought that the Darwins of today
may be known to posterity only in the case-books of the
psychiatrists.

Many intriguing cases like Darwin's can be cited. Pickering believes that Sigmund Freud, the founder of psychoanalysis, also suffered from a severe psychoneurosis, particularly during his most creative period. Freud was afflicted with all sorts of fears and imaginary ailments at that time.

But individual cases are not necessarily representative. There are, after all, plenty of deeply troubled bank clerks, housewives, gas station attendants, and high school teachers. Highly creative people, like Darwin, also tend to be highly visible. Wealthy and prominent people may also be allowed the luxury of indulging their behavioral oddities. Ordinary folk could not retire to the country as Darwin did. And how many potentially creative individuals may have been destroyed by mental illness?

What is needed is a general statistical survey. The first attempt at this was made by the English psychologist Havelock Ellis. He chose 1,030 names out of the *Dictionary of National Biography*, a listing of prominent people in Britain. Though Ellis thought he could discern some slight relationship between creativity and mental illness, he concludes, "we must put out of court any theory as to genius being a form of insanity."

Other studies tend to confirm Ellis's conclusion. All studies of the possible relationship between creativity and mental illness have been criticized as suffering from "softness" of data and an inability to properly define either creativity or mental illness. Still they represent the best efforts of social scientists from a number of countries, and the conclusions cannot easily be put aside.

Psychiatrists E. Slater and A. Meyer, who reviewed the studies, conclude that they represent "a decisive counter-demonstration to the vulgar belief that men of genius are by and large mad or half-mad, and it shows that not only is normality of personality compatible with the highest achievement but also that the majority of men of the greatest achievement are normal."

And Pickering, who set out to study *Creative Malady*, concludes, "This general survey suggests that there is no strong connection between mental illness and creativity."

Both drug addiction and alcoholism have often been linked in popular opinion with creativity. Drugs and alcohol can produce states in which ordinary ways of viewing reality are shattered. Poets often write about how wine inspires them. "Wine, true begetter of all arts that be," wrote Hilaire Belloc. In recent years, however, alcohol has not often been viewed as an aid to creativity. There have been a large number of highly creative individuals who have become alcoholics, but their addiction has been regarded as a problem not an inspiration. There is also no evidence that creative people become alcoholics more frequently than noncreative people.

During the 1960s powerful psychoactive or mind altering drugs like LSD virtually exploded on the American social scene. The drugs were capable of producing stunning mind altering effects, vivid hallucinations, feelings of mystic unity and of absolute terror.

At first drugs like LSD were described as "conscious-ness expanding," and there was a good deal of talk that they might "liberate" the mind for creative endeavor. A number of artists, musicians, and writers reported exper-imenting with the drugs.

The reaction of conventional society to these psychoac-tive drugs was swift and harsh. They were banned, and the users of even mildly psychoactive substances like marijuana were subject to savage penalties. Most re-search with drugs like LSD was stopped cold.

But there was very little evidence that psychoactive drugs actually stimulated creativity. Creative people of-ten moved in groups where experimentation with drugs was more common. Much of the presumed relationship between the psychoactive drugs and creativity appears to have been the result of an early romantic enthusiasm for the drugs. But without further legitimate research we will never know for sure.

A century earlier there had been the same sort of enthusiasm for opium and its derivatives. These sub-stances were freely available and often given out as pain killers or sleeping potions. A large number of people became addicted to opium before medical men real-ized what was happening and use of the drug was cur-tailed.

Like LSD opium in some forms is capable of producing vivid and strange images. The most famous of the opium-induced poems was "Kubla Khan" by Samuel Taylor Coleridge. He was said to have awakened from a sleep induced by laudanum, a liquid form of opium, with the poem fully formed in his mind. While feverishly writing the poem down, Coleridge was interrupted by an inconvenient caller and was never able to recapture the exact tone of his drug-induced visions.

But, as with LSD, there is no compelling evidence that opium in any form induces creativity. One poem—even a good one—out of the entire history of poetry is not much on which to base a theory.

5

Measuring Creativity

For the longest time the idea of testing for creativity seemed an absurd notion, almost a sacrilegious one. Even today the idea is not entirely accepted. Often it is resented as an attempt to confine the free spirit of creativity. But the idea is no longer thought to be entirely absurd.

It took a change in our notion of creativity to produce a change in our attitude toward testing it. So long as creativity was regarded as a special gift from God or the sole property of genius, it seemed hopeless to try to test for it. It seemed as hopeless as trying to test for other desirable qualities like goodness or beauty. Such qualities could be generally recognized, but they could not be measured or even adequately described.

The same problems arose if creativity were a form of madness, as some cynics contended. In this view, creativity was no longer a desirable trait, but it was still something that appeared only very rarely.

Over the last century, however, a more democratic and cheerful view of creativity has come into vogue. Creativity is now widely regarded as the property, to a greater or lesser degree, of every person. Once that idea is adopted, it is possible, at least in theory, to measure creativity. If creativity is no longer thought of as a spontaneous "gift" but as a universal human trait, it can then be defined, located, and measured. Statistical techniques used to measure other human characteristics (like intelligence, for example) can be brought into play.

The idea that human attributes like creativity could be measured began with the nineteenth-century British thinker Sir Francis Galton. Galton was the perfect Victorian gentleman-scientist. He was wealthy, energetic, widely read, well traveled, and curious about almost everything. He had the Victorian's faith that all problems were approachable through scientific inquiry. He also came from a distinguished family: Charles Darwin was his cousin.

One of the problems which occupied Galton's probing mind was why some men seemed to succeed so spectacularly in life while others failed miserably. (The term "men" by the way, was not used as a general description of all humanity. To Galton it meant only the male of the species. The notion that women could contribute anything other than male children to the advancement of civilization was utterly foreign to most thinkers of Galton's time.)

Galton collected information on all the famous and successful people he could find. From his studies he produced a very influential work called *Hereditary Genius*. It was Galton's theory that every human being inherited a capacity called "general intelligence." Geniuses were those with an exceptionally high degree of this all-around mental capacity. The primary controlling factor of this capacity was heredity. Galton's evidence indicated that genius ran in families.

In Galton's view, the best way to produce geniuses was to breed for them, the same way that we breed prize cattle and dogs. Galton's study led to the development of eugenics, the presumed science of human breeding. It also led, though less directly, to the development of intelligence testing.

Galton's ideas have had an unhappy history. Eugenics was eventually picked up by the Nazis in Germany. They tried to breed a "master race" and eliminate "inferior" races. (Even IQ tests have been widely denounced as "racist" in recent years.) His own theories and statistics were often naive. But Francis Galton was undeniably a pioneer in the field of measuring human mental abilities.

Galton was not only a theoretician. For years he conducted a variety of tests of human abilities in his London laboratory. His tests seem primitive today and wide of the mark, but at least he had begun the task of trying to put some sort of statistical order into the jumble of human abilities.

In *Hereditary Genius*, Galton did not single out a factor of creativity. Original or creative ideas were just part of general intelligence to Galton. But later in his life (Galton lived to be very vigorous eighty-nine) he modified his original theory somewhat. In addition to general intelligence, Galton came to lay almost equal stress on other qualities, which he also thought were primarily hereditary. Of these special qualities the most important was what he called "fluency," that is, "an unusual and spontaneous flow of images and ideas." He saw such minds "always pullulating with new notions." Today we would call "fluency" creativity.

Galton never developed adequate tests for "fluency" any more than he did for "general intelligence." What he did do was forcefully introduce the novel notion that such qualities could be tested for. He removed the quality of "genius" from the realm of the divine and mystical and made it human.

Intelligence testing began in France around the turn of the century. IQ testing on a mass scale began in the U.S. during the first World War. But it wasn't until the 1950s that creativity tests were developed and used widely.

Intelligence testing has grown into a virtual industry, particularly in the United States. Today intelligence testing is extremely influential in education and other fields though it is also highly controversial. IQ tests have severe critics and passionate defenders.

But even the most enthusiastic proponents of creativity testing admit that such tests are still in their infancy, and that they leave a lot to be desired. Often the tests produce contradictory or ambiguous results. Critics of the tests claim that they are of no value whatever, and, worse, that they tend to stifle creativity by putting limits on it. But since they are not as widely used as IQ tests and are not nearly as influential, they have not kicked up as much controversy either.

Effective or not, such tests represent a serious attempt to get a handle on the elusive quality that we call creativity. We will look in more detail at some of these tests and the results that they have produced.

Creativity tests didn't grow in a vacuum. They began in earnest in the 1950s in response to social and political conditions. Mass IQ testing began in the first World War because the Army wanted to know more about the huge number of new men it suddenly had to deal with. In 1957, the Soviet Union orbited the world's first space satellite. For many years the U.S. had been secure in its belief that it had the most advanced and productive scientific community in the world. The security was based on the assumption that American freedom stimulated scientific creativity, whereas the repressive Soviet system stifled it. Therefore it seemed impossible that the Soviets could ever equal, and certainly not surpass, U.S. scientific achievement. *Sputnik I* destroyed that comfortable security.

All sorts of disturbing information was published about the large number of scientists and engineers that the Soviet Union was training. There was a growing feeling that if the U.S. didn't change its ways, it would fall behind. Freedom of inquiry was not enough.

One result of this post-*Sputnik* fright was an enormous increase in the amount of money that was put into education, particularly scientific education. Another was a hurried attempt to understand the nature of creativity and the creative person and to develop tests which would identify such individuals, particularly in the area of science. The hope was that potentially valuable scientists could be spotted early in life and receive the proper training and encouragement.

Since no one has been able to agree on a definition of creativity, how can you construct a test for it? And once you have a test, how can you verify the results; that is, how do you know it is the genuinely creative people who are getting the high scores?

What most test compilers did was this: they put together a series of questions or tasks that they assumed a creative person would do well on. Next they chose a target group, for example, a group of high school students or the scientists working at a large corporation. They had teachers or supervisors rate the students or scientists as to their creative ability. Then they gave that group the test. If those rated as creative scored better than those rated as not creative, the test maker could assume that he was on the right track.

Questions were changed and refined in accordance with the results of earlier tests. Tests were then checked with other groups and compared with the results of other creativity tests to see how great or small a correlation existed. Results were also checked against a host of other data such as economic status and the results of IQ tests. This process of validating creativity tests (or any other behavioral or psychological test for that matter) is lengthy and complex. It results in volumes of statistics and thousands upon thousands of yards of computer printouts.

When compiled and examined, the test results are printed up in learned journals replete with graphs and charts and festooned with footnotes. It all looks very solid and unassailable, like the statistics on annual world steel production. But it isn't solid at all, as the testers themselves sometimes reluctantly admit.

Among students, the most commonly used tests for creative thinking grew out of psychologist J. P. Guilford's Unusual Uses Test. Guilford asked his subjects, "Think of as many unusual uses of a brick as you can." They were then given a time limit, and those who compiled the longest lists in the specified time were considered to have given the most creative answers.

There were no "correct" answers to such questions. The answers didn't even have to be reasonable in the ordinary sense of that word. For example, one response that was cited by psychologists as creative was to use the brick as a "bug hider." "Put the brick on the ground for a week, then pick it up and look at the bugs hiding under it."

A whole series of creativity tests was developed under the direction of E. P. Torrance for the University of Minnesota. They are known collectively as the Minnesota Tests and have been the most widely used of the creativity tests. Many of them are based on the Guilford model.

A popular test of the Minnesota type is to ask children to imagine an impossible situation and what the consequences might be.

What would happen if man could be invisible at will?

What would happen if a hole could be bored through the earth?

What would happen if the language of birds and animals could be understood by man?

Students had a five-minute time limit to make their lists.

These tests were adequate for children in the fifth grade and above when reading and writing skills were fairly well developed. For lower grades tests were developed which didn't require language skills. In some the children were handed a toy and asked how they could improve it. Once again the more suggestions, the higher the creativity score.

Another Minnesota test for school age children is called

the Incomplete Figures Task. The subject is presented with ten incomplete figures, for example, parallel lines or a pair of semicircles. He is then asked to sketch some subject or design "that no one else in the class will think of." The subjects are asked to write in the name of the object they have sketched or, for the very young, have the titles they suggest written in by the teacher.

Here is how the test is scored: one point is given for each drawing completed. If the subject makes ten drawings, he gets ten points. He gets one point for each category used in completing the figures. If, for example, he makes three drawings of flowers he gets only one point for all three. One or two points on each drawing can be awarded for originality. The drawings are checked against those made by a sample group. If less than 5 percent of the sample made a similar drawing one point is given, if less than 2 percent, 2 points. Finally one point is given for every important detail in each drawing.

Another test is called the Circles Task. Thirty-six small circles are printed on a sheet of paper. The subjects are asked to draw as many objects as possible in which a circle is the main element. The task is scored in the same manner as the picture completion task.

Tests that depend more on language, like the Ask and Guess Test, are also used. In this test the subject is shown a picture of a nursery rhyme story like "Tom, Tom, the Piper's Son." They are then asked to do several things. First to ask as many questions about the picture as they can think of; to state as many possible causes of the events depicted in the picture, and finally to give as many consequences or results as they can of the action depicted.

In another test, the subject is given relatively unfamiliar sounds and asked to write down images and ideas associated with each of the sounds.

In yet another test, students are handed a list of topics and given twenty minutes to write a story about one of them. The topics are things like "The dog that doesn't bark," "The man who cries," "The lion that doesn't roar," and "The flying monkey." The stories are scored on a very detailed and complex scale that is supposed to take into account such factors as originality, interest, and general creativity.

These Minnesota tests and many others like them have run into a variety of problems. They have not turned out to be nearly as useful as their original compilers had hoped. In the first place, the tests are difficult to administer. A major criticism of the tests is that creativity cannot be turned on and off in a ten-minute time limit. Often it takes a period of deliberation to come up with an original idea. Those who do well may merely be fast, which is not necessarily the same as being creative. There seems no way around this problem in a test situation.

Scoring is another major problem. No matter how many standardized graphs and tables a scorer is given, a good deal of scoring ultimately comes down to the scorer's individual subjective judgment. There are no clearly right or wrong answers in such tests. A technical problem is that scoring such tests is tedious and time consuming. That increases the cost of administering the test.

The contents of the tests have been severely criticized. Those who compile them have a general theory of what elements make up creativity. These include such factors as finding similarities between unlike things and differences between things that seem alike. But not everyone agrees with the tester's analysis of creative thinking. Torrance's reply to this criticism is, essentially, that we are doing the best we can with what we know.

Finally, the tests have been criticized as trivial. Is a student going to be inspired to creative endeavor by a brick? The response is that students who take the tests are generally enthusiastic and enjoy them.

While those who do well on such tests are generally those who are also regarded as creative by their teachers and fellow students, the tests don't provide much additional information. Critics wonder why it is necessary to go through all the trouble and expense of administering a test, if you can get essentially the same sort of information just by asking others.

Another approach to the measurement of creativity is to first identify creative individuals (usually by asking teachers or supervisors) and then test them to see what particular characteristics they have in common. This approach has been tried many times with varying and sometimes contradictory results.

One assumption that had persisted, at least since the days of Galton, was that a highly creative person must necessarily also be a highly intelligent person. But in the 1950s and '60s a variety of studies brought that assumption into question. The studies indicated that "intelligence," at least as measured on standard IQ tests, could not be directly related to creativity.

Frank Barron, a professor of psychology at the University of California, notes in his influential book *The Creative Person*, "The relationship between intelligence and creativity . . . is . . . by no means a simple one."

A great deal depended upon the field in which the creativity was being exercised. In some areas like mathematics and physics there was a correlation between creativity and IQ, but even here the correlation was in Barron's opinion "quite low."

Among artists such as painters, sculptors, and designers there was no correlation at all between IQ scores and the rated quality of their work. Indeed, those with lower IQs tended to do slightly better in the creativity ratings.

Does that mean that there was such a thing as the low IQ, highly creative person? Not necessarily, because these findings were based on studies of people already at work in their various fields. Barron points out, "It must be remembered that commitment to such [creative] endeavors is already selective for intelligence, so that the average IQ is already a superior one."

Even with those qualifications, not all psychologists agree with Barron's conclusions about the lack of relationship between creativity and IQ. Other studies dispute Barron's results or at least tend to blur the conclusions. Still there remains the genuine possibility that what we call creativity and what we call intelligence are not inextricably linked together, particularly in the arts.

Popular stereotype holds that the highly creative person is also highly eccentric. Psychological testing tends to back up this stereotype—at least to the extent of indicating that creative people are less conventional in their attitudes than less creative people.

Psychologists Jacob Getzels and Philip Jackson did a whole series of tests and studies of what were considered "highly gifted" students. The students were divided into two categories, those who had high IQs but were not rated as highly creative, and those who were highly creative but did not necessarily have high IQs. Both groups had IQs which averaged above the national average of 100. The high creativity group had a mean IQ of 127, the high intelligence group a mean IQ of 150. Both groups were also superior in their schoolwork but for different reasons.

When asked what occupations they were considering the high IQs gave conventional answers like lawyer, doctor, professor, and so forth. The high creatives went for more unconventional occupations like adventurer, inventor, and writer. Sixty-two percent of the high creatives made unconventional choices, whereas only 16 percent of the high IQs did.

The two groups were given picture tests: they were shown a fairly simple drawing and asked to make up a story about it. The high creatives responded with more unconventional stories. Write Getzels and Jackson in *Creativity and Intelligence*:

> The high creatives tend to free themselves from the stimulus [the picture] using it largely as a point of departure for self-expression. . . . The picture stimulus may be of a man in an airplane, but the story he wants to tell is about a divorce, the picture stimulus may be of a man alone in an office, but the story he wants to tell is of a private eye in a cereal factory. . . . The high creativity adolescent has a more playful—or if you will, more experimental—attitude toward conventional ideas, objects, and qualities.

The importance of playfulness, even humor, often crops up in discussions of creativity. It also cropped up in the tests administered by Getzels and Jackson to their two groups. When asked to draw a picture of a particular subject, the high creative group responded with a significantly higher degree of humor than did the high IQ group.

In one test, the students were asked to draw a picture appropriate to the title "Playing Tag in the School Yard." The instructions said "You may draw any picture you like—whatever you may imagine for this theme."

Two examples published with the study display a dramatic contrast. The picture drawn by the high IQ student shows students playing tag in the school yard just like the title says. The picture drawn by the highly creative student shows no children playing tag, indeed no school yard. It shows what appears to be the front of a graffiti-covered school with broken windows. Some of the graffiti read "Down With the Faculty," "Bolivian Revolution," "I Hate Children," and "No, I'm Not Mature, Are You?" A little note in the corner explains "It is ghosts who are playing tag."

Now, such unconventional and distinctly rebellious attitudes as expressed in the drawing may lead to trouble with authority. Getzels and Jackson found that it did. When teachers were asked to rate students as to the degree they enjoyed having them in class, the high IQ students were rated as more desirable than the ordinary students, but the high creative students were not.

Psychologist Anne Roe, quoted in the book *Human Behavior*, concluded that highly creative adolescents

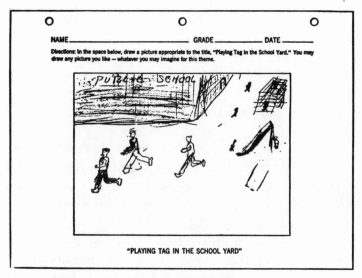

Test pictures on the theme of "Playing Tag in the School Yard," produced by high I.Q. student (above), and high creative student (below).

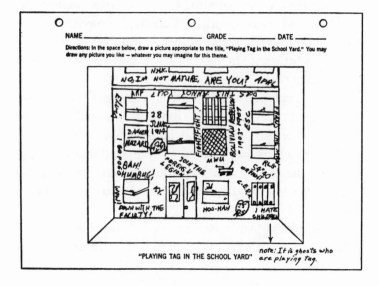

would tend to get into more scrapes with authority than their less creative peers.

> These conflicts may become particularly acute in the children we are concerned with, because they are very bright. Many of them are brighter than their teachers, and they can think up a lot of things that are very difficult for their teachers to cope with.

Tests of people rated as highly creative indicate that they show a marked preference for the complex, the novel, and that they are interested in situations that contain a puzzle or mystery to be solved rather than those that are straightforward.

Barron found that when highly creative people and less creative people were shown drawings, the creative people liked the complicated and often unbalanced drawings. They preferred tests in which they could participate rather than tests in which they merely had to make a choice. But while they apparently liked disorder, they appeared to want to impose their own idea of order upon it.

Barron writes:

> Perhaps the single most well-established conclusion to which our work has led, not only with writers but with other artists and with scientists as well, concerns the creative individual's response to apparent disorder and his own need to find a subtle ordering principle.

In a study of architects, Donald W. McKinnon found that those who were highly creative displayed a distinct "liking of the rich, complex and asymmetrical."

The Rorschach inkblot test is a standard psychological test. The subject is shown a shapeless inkblot and asked what it looks like. From the responses, the psychologist attempts to draw some conclusions about the subject's personality. Highly creative people tend to respond differently to the Rorschach test than others. Says Barron:

> When confronted, for instance, with the Rorschach inkblot test, original [creative] individuals insist to a most uncommon degree upon giving an interpretation of the blot which takes account of all details in one comprehensive, synthesizing image.

What has over two decades of attempting to measure the elusive quality of creativity revealed to us? Not a great deal that is new, and nothing that is undisputed. Primarily the tests have tended to back up previously held common sense judgments; for example, that "intelligence" as defined in IQ tests is not synonymous with creativity, and that creative people tend to be more hostile to authority and impatient with traditional restraints.

The tests have in no sense been unqualified successes —no psychological or behavioral tests have—but they have not been total failures either. Since creativity remains such a valued yet little understood quality, attempts to measure it will undoubtedly continue.

6

Nature versus Nurture

One controversy which affects almost all branches of the behavioral sciences is that of nature versus nurture. That is to say, how much of any particular human quality is due to an individual's heredity and how much comes from the environment in which he or she was raised? Inevitably, the subject of creativity is right in the middle of the controversy.

As we saw in the previous chapter, Galton, from whom we can date the study of creativity, came down very firmly on the side of nature. When he studied the family trees of eminent men, he found that they had a great proportion of eminent relatives. The more outstanding the individual, Galton found, the more likely he was to have outstanding relatives.

Galton writes:

The general uniformity in the distribution of ability among the kinsmen in the different groups, is strikingly manifest.

The eminent sons are almost invariably more numerous than the eminent brothers, and those are a trifle more numerous than the eminent fathers. On proceeding further down the table we come to a sudden dropping off in the numbers at the second grade of kinship, namely, at the grandfather, uncles, nephews, and grandsons. . . . On reaching the third grade of kinship, another abrupt dropping off in numbers is again met with, but the first cousins are found to occupy a decidedly better position than other relations within the third grade.

Wasn't it possible that the sons and close relatives of eminent men had far greater opportunities to achieve high positions than other people did, particularly in a society like Victorian England which had a rigid class structure? Galton certainly did not think so. He was absolutely sure that people rose to prominence because of their inherited abilities.

I feel convinced that no man can achieve a very high reputation without being gifted with very high abilities and I trust that reason has been given for the belief, that few who possess these very high abilities can fail in achieving eminence.

In this Galton reflected the prevailing view of his times, which held that successful people deserved their success, and unsuccessful people deserved failure.

At the other extreme of the argument were some twentieth-century social scientists who argued that children were very much like soft clay. They could be shaped or molded by their environment in an endless variety of ways. One social scientist said that if he were given six healthy infants and an entirely free hand in raising them he could make one a successful doctor, another a lawyer, a third a painter, and so forth. Such theories became popular in the U.S. during the 1930s and '40s and reflected the more democratic and optimistic outlook of the times.

These extreme positions are not widely held today, yet the argument goes on between those who wish to place most emphasis on heredity and those who favor environment. There is a practical side to the argument. If creativity is largely hereditary, there is very little we can do to encourage it. If environment is the key then it is worthwhile trying to develop educational programs which stimulate creativity.

Though Galton believed that he was making a scientific statistical survey of eminent people, we can recognize today that his statistics were primitive. No universally accepted way has ever been found of separating heredity from environmental influences in a statistical survey. In fact no universally accepted way has been found of deciding who is eminent. Galton dipped into the pages of the *Dictionary of National Biography* for his list. Not everyone would agree he used the best method.

One of the most important arguments on the nature side of the question is the existence of child prodigies. If a very young child displays enormous ability, this would argue strongly for the importance of heredity. The abilities of a child prodigy develop before the environment can have too great an effect.

But the stories of child prodigies are exaggerated. There are, in fact, only three fields in which there have been genuine child prodigies: music, mathematics, and chess.

Mozart was an accomplished performer on several instruments before the age of six.

Mozart is the most celebrated of the musical prodigies. He was an accomplished performer on several instruments before the age of six and composed symphonies before he was sixteen.

Karl Friedrich Gauss's (1777-1855) mathematics teachers soon recognized that their young pupil knew more than they did or ever would. He was making important original mathematical discoveries while still in his teens, and many today regard Gauss as one of the three greatest mathematicians that ever lived.

Chess has seen a string of child prodigies. The eccentric Bobby Fischer, who was a chess grandmaster at the age of fourteen and considered the best player in the world while still in his early twenties, is only one example of a chess prodigy. Paul Charles Morphy, who won the world chess title in 1858 at age twenty-one, was another.

These three fields do have some basic similarities, since both music and chess can be analyzed mathematically. In other fields child prodigies really don't exist. Some poets have done their best work while quite young, but not as children.

There are definite differences in age for the most creative periods of individuals in different fields. But a study by Harvey Lehman, published by Princeton University, found that in general most highly creative work, be it artistic, scientific, or scholarly, was produced fairly early—usually while the creative individual was still in his thirties.

According to Lehman's survey, before the age of thirty, chemists and poets were likely to do their most creative work. Between thirty and thirty-four, mathematicians, symphonic composers (prodigies were too rare to have

*Bobby Fischer was U.S. Chess Champion
at the age of fourteen.*

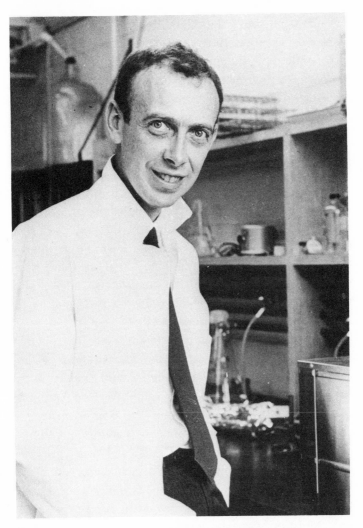

*James D. Watson helped to crack the riddle of the
DNA molecule when he was only twenty-five.*

any effect on these statistics), botanists, and physicists were most creative. Between thirty-five and thirty-nine, astronomers, physiologists, philosophers, and composers of opera did their most creative work. Only novelists and architects tended to work most creatively after forty, according to the Lehman survey.

The decline of creative abilities is one of the great puzzles to those who have studied the subject. As an individual accumulates more knowledge and experience, it would seem that he should be able to continue to be creative, indeed that he should become more so. Certainly there is no measurable decline in the powers of the brain after age forty. And there are always exceptions. Some of the greatest figures in any field are those who continued to work creatively for many years. But over all, the fact is that most important creative work is done early in a career if it is to be done at all.

James D. Watson was only twenty-five when along with Francis Crick he figured out the structure of the DNA molecule. He has been called a child prodigy, but a twenty-five year old is no longer a child. Watson's account of the epic discovery in his book *The Double Helix* is a sharp and irreverent description of scientific creativity and of the politics of science. Crick's and Watson's great rival in this race to solve the DNA puzzle was American biochemist Linus Pauling. A race is really what it was. Everyone knew the problem would be solved soon, the only question was who would do it first and reap the honor. Pauling was over fifty at that time and was considered a phenomenon in the scientific community because he was still doing highly creative work, and because he was still a threat to be the first to find the molecular structure of DNA.

I have spoken to many scientists; like athletes they fear turning forty. While they can certainly continue to do scientific work and accumulate honors, they think their time of great creative productivity is over. Statistics back up this fear.

What happens? Why does creativity decline in so many fields so early in life?

One of the hallmarks of the creative person is the ability to look at a problem in a new way; neurologist Wilder Penfield calls it a "fresh brain." After a certain point in life it appears that for most people the mind is too set, too cluttered with preconceptions, premature conclusions, and patterned responses. Is this a biological process—the formation of certain fixed neural pathways in the brain? Or is it without physical basis—simply the habit of thinking in a particular manner or a way of life which does not allow time for creative work? In short, is it nature or nurture?

Another major puzzle in the study of creativity is the apparent existence of clusters of creativity. It seems that the human race moves along at a fairly steady pace for long periods and then quite suddenly there is a creative outburst which witnesses the flowering of a great number of new ideas.

The first of these intensively creative periods that we can discern took place in ancient Egypt about six thousand years ago. For centuries, mankind had lived in small communities doing relatively simple farming. Buildings, such as they were, were constructed from mud brick. Around the year 2700 B.C. the first free-standing stone structure that we know of was built. Called the step pyramid, it was a tomb for an early king of Egypt. Within a little over a century, building techniques had progressed to the point that the Great Pyramid could be constructed. The Great Pyramid is still one of the architectural wonders of the world, the largest free-standing stone structure ever built.

In the period just preceding the construction of the step pyramid, Egypt had been changed from a scattering of small independent kingdoms into a single unified state. The Egyptian state, by the way, lasted longer than any other in history. Massive irrigation projects were begun for the first time. The same period also saw the introduction of the hieroglyphic form of writing.

By any measure these are extraordinary achievements. Tradition (for the records we possess from that time can hardly be called history) attributes many of these achievements to a single individual, Imhotep. Historians agree that there almost certainly was a real Imhotep, and that he probably designed the step pyramid. Whether he also introduced writing or did many of the other things which legends say he did, is doubtful. Later, Imhotep was considered a god and worshiped by the Egyptians. Today archeologists believe they may be close to discovering his tomb near the step pyramid. Imhotep is the first creative genius that we can identify.

Fifth century B.C. Athens is another of those periods in history that seems to stand out as an era of remarkable creativity. It is often called the Golden Age of Greece. A third era is Italy during the fourteenth and early fifteenth centuries—the time known as the Renaissance. And others could be added to this list.

Is it possible that through some unknown biological mechanism there is a greater concentration of the genes for creative genius at certain times and certain places? Possible, but highly unlikely. Nothing that we know about the distribution of hereditary characteristics would support such an explanation.

It is far more reasonable to believe that the genetic possibility for creativity exists in about the same proportion throughout history, and that special social circumstances allow it to flourish at particular times. In ancient Egypt, these circumstances may have been the unification of the entire country under a single monarch. This feat created the conditions for all of the other developments which followed.

No matter how great the genius of Imhotep, he would quite obviously never have been able to build a pyramid single-handed or with a small crew. What was needed was a large and disciplined work force, and this would become available only under a strong central government. There would have been no need for a pyramid unless there was a god-king to bury inside.

A large disciplined work force would also have been necessary for the construction of irrigation projects. Irrigation would have increased the food supply. An increased food supply and increased wealth would have given the Egyptians both the time and the resources to plan other major projects. No society which lives at a bare subsistence level can be expected to produce many creative individuals since in a primitive society practically all of a person's time and energy is taken up in the struggle for survival. There is precious little time left over to engage in a search for new solutions to problems.

Primitive societies are also usually extremely traditional. They do not welcome new ideas. But primitive societies are not alone in clinging to tradition; many advanced cultures are hostile to innovation. Had Michelangelo been born among the Muslims he would never have been able to create his David or to paint the Sistine Chapel ceiling, though the Muslims of the time were a highly civilized people. He would never even have thought of such projects since the Muslim religion forbids all representations of the human form.

One of the great unresolvable arguments of all times runs something like this: If Napoleon had been born on a South Sea island, would he still have been a great general? Turned around, the argument is equally unresolvable. If Napoleon had not been born at all, would the history of Europe have been greatly changed?

While periods like the Renaissance seem to stand out from the pages of history, we must also keep in mind the possibility that we exaggerate the significance of these creative periods. We often ignore the enormous amount of vital groundwork for any creative outburst that was laid beforehand.

We also have to recognize that an atmosphere in which creativity flourishes tends to attract creative people from many places. In the 1940s and '50s, the United States was the unquestioned leader in world science. There were many fine native American scientists, but many foreign scientists had been attracted to the U.S. by the large number of well-financed laboratories and institutions which could support their work. Many others had been driven to the U.S. by the Nazi domination of Europe.

While what we call creativity may be present to some degree in all of us, there is a general impression that a relatively small number of individuals are responsible for the majority of creative contributions. A study by sociologist Wayne Dennis seems to bear out this impression. Dennis found that in seven diverse fields including music, geology, and chemistry, the top 10 percent of contributors produced about 50 percent of the work.

Another subject which crops up in any discussion of creativity is the phenomenon of simultaneous discovery: two individuals who independently come up with the same unique idea at the same time. History or tradition holds that there are a large number of important simultaneous discoveries, probably the most famous being the "simultaneous" discovery by Darwin and Wallace of the theory of evolution. But, as we explained in an earlier chapter, the discovery was not really simultaneous at all. Darwin had hit upon the idea eighteen years before Wallace thought of it but for his own reasons had delayed publication.

In fact, Darwin didn't really discover the theory of evolution at all. The idea that one species had evolved from another had been around for a long time. Darwin's own grandfather, Erasmus Darwin, had written on the subject. What Charles Darwin and Wallace had added was a theory of the mechanism of evolution—the how and the why of the evolution of the species. Their idea was natural selection—the survival of the fittest. Both Darwin and Wallace had undergone similar experiences; both had traveled widely observing and collecting plants and animals. Darwin had circled the world on the *Beagle*. Wallace had spent time collecting in South America and was in the Malay archipelago when he hit upon his theory. Both men had been inspired by reading Thomas Malthus's essay *On Population*. Malthus said that population would quickly outgrow the food supply, and that the only way that the two would be brought back into line was by famine and disease. In hindsight, the leap from Malthus to Darwin and Wallace does not seem very great. When Darwin's contemporary Thomas Henry Huxley first read Darwin's theory he was struck by its utter simplicity. "By God, why didn't I think of that?" he exclaimed. Often great ideas do seem simple—once the proper connections are made.

When the circumstances are known, there is nothing mysterious or supernatural about the phenomenon of simultaneous discovery. The groundwork had already been laid. If Darwin had not hit upon the idea then it would have been Wallace, and if not Wallace then someone else. Neither Darwin nor Wallace possessed utterly unique qualities of mind. How much different the history of science might have been if one or the other of them had not existed is impossible to say. But it seems safe enough to conclude that the theory of evolution by natural selection would have been hit upon by someone, even if there never had been a Darwin or a Wallace.

In addressing the nature-nurture controversy, educational psychologist E. Paul Torrance made a statement (which appears in the collection *Explorations in Creativity*) with which most of his colleagues would probably agree:

In Ancient Greece, the philosopher Plato declared that "what is honored in a country will be cultivated there." Plato surely must have included creative talents among the things that are nurtured by honoring them in a culture. The prevailing concept, however, is that creativity must be left to chance, and that if one has outstanding creative talent, it will somehow flourish in spite of neglect and abuse. This erroneous idea has dominated thinking even among educators, in spite of the mass of contradictory evidence. No one would argue, of course, that hereditary factors do not place limits upon creative development and achievement. Creative abilities are inherited to the extent that a person inherits his sense organs, a peripheral nervous system, and a brain. How these abilities develop and function, however, is strongly influenced by the way the environment responds to a person's curiosity and creative needs.

A variety of attempts has been made to increase creativity—usually through educational techniques. Even the best of these attempts can only be considered very limited successes. Perhaps the techniques themselves are faulty or perhaps the belief is false that creativity can be deliberately nurtured and encouraged. But then again Plato may have pointed out the real crux of the problem when he said, "What is honored *in a country* will be cultivated there." There is a lot more to a country than its schools.

Let us take, as an example, a school program which encourages creativity in art. How much effect will this have in a family or community which regards art as an inconsequential waste of time or even suspects it of being somehow strange and abnormal? How much effect will it have in a larger society which does not have a high regard for artists, and in which artists have an extremely difficult time making a living?

While the nurture of creative abilities on a mass scale may in fact be possible, it is no small task. It is probably well beyond the powers of the educational system alone.

7

Dreaming and Creativity

In 1865 the German organic chemist Friedrich August Kekulé was pondering a very difficult problem. What was the atomic structure of the chemical benzene? Benzene was proving to be an important element in the chemical makeup of newly created synthetic dyes. Without a proper idea of its structure, progress could be slowed considerably.

So Kekulé, already a world renowned chemist, turned his attention to the puzzle, but without much success at first. Then one day while he was riding a bus he dozed off and began to dream. In the dream he saw atoms whirling in a dance. Suddenly the tail end of one chain attached itself to the head end "like a snake eating its tail." In Kekulé's dream the atoms formed a spinning ring.

As a dignified German professor, Kekulé could not jump off the bus and run down the street shouting "Eureka," as Archimedes is reported to have done. But he did not forget his dream either. In due time he published a scientific paper which suggested that the atomic structure of benzene was a ring. The suggestion proved to be correct.

The story of how Kekulé cracked the atomic structure of benzene has been retold many times, often in a more dramatic and exaggerated fashion. It still remains an excellent example of how dreaming or daydreaming can be used by the mind to solve a problem—to create. Kekulé's experience was not a unique or even unusual one.

The American inventor Elias Howe was confronted with an apparently insoluble problem while attempting to develop the sewing machine. Then he had a dream about spears. This suggested to him the idea of putting the eye at the bottom of the sewing machine needle rather than at the top. The idea was an absolutely crucial one.

Robert Louis Stevenson said that the inspiration for his story *Dr. Jekyll and Mr. Hyde* came to him in a dream. Bram Stoker said he first conceived of *Dracula* in a nightmare.

The list of examples of creative dreams reported by famous people can be extended to great length. But we don't need the testimony of highly creative scientists, writers, or artists in order to realize that there appears to be some relationship between creativity and dreaming. When confronted with a difficult problem many of us decide to "sleep on it."

To a degree sleeping on a problem is simply a way to avoid making an immediate decision—but it also works. I'm sure that many of you have gone to bed worried about a problem and awakened the next morning with a solution or at least with a new perspective that led to a solution. Perhaps the solution didn't come to you in a dream like

Robert Louis Stevenson: Dr. Jekyll and Mr. Hyde came to him in a dream.

Kekulé's circle of atoms—at least not a dream that you can remember. But it seems clear that during sleep the mind was at work somehow on the problem.

Lying awake thinking about a problem doesn't help at all—indeed it generally makes things worse. There is a point at which the conscious mind no longer has any useful effect upon a problem.

As long as creativity was regarded as something spontaneous and rather mysterious, dreams seemed the perfect vehicle for creative inspiration. Until recent times, dreams themselves have been regarded as unpredictable and rather mysterious mental events.

In ancient times some people thought that sleep was a period during which the soul was able to leave the body and wander about the universe. Dreams, they believed, were the partial memories of the soul's nightly wanderings.

Many societies, including that of the ancient Hebrews, thought that sleep was a time in which God could talk directly to men. Prophecies received in dreams were taken very seriously indeed. Interpreting dreams was regarded a highly skilled and valued art. Even kings paid heed to messages received in dreams.

In a few societies individuals were almost ruled by their dreams. That never happened in Western history, but still dreams were at times given a great deal of weight. The general impression was that during sleep the soul or the mind could come in contact with forces greater than itself.

The seventeenth and eighteenth centuries saw the growth of rationalism and the scientific method in Europe and America. Dreams which were irrational and beyond scientific investigation fell sharply in esteem. They were thought to be something insubstantial and unrelated to real life. A dream, no longer a message from God, was now thought of as something thoroughly impractical. When someone was being unrealistic he was called "a dreamer." It was not a compliment.

At the start of the twentieth century, the attitude toward dreams changed once again. This time the change was the result of the work of Sigmund Freud, father of psychoanalysis. In Freud's very influential opinion, dreams were messages from our unconscious minds. They were little nightly dramas in which we acted out some of our buried desires and fantasies—usually sexual in nature. Sleep lowered the conscious mind's barriers to unthinkable thoughts. Freud made dream interpretation one of the most important parts of his treatment of mental illness.

Freud even attempted an analysis of the creative genius of Leonardo da Vinci, primarily by interpreting a dream that the fourteenth-century Italian had once reported.

The theories of Freud and his followers were elegant and popular but entirely speculative. They had a small number of case histories but no hard statistics and no scientifically acceptable measurements to support their ideas.

Hard science didn't really get into the subject of sleep and dreams until the late 1950s. Once it did though, the result was an entirely new and unexpected view of the one-third of our life that we spend asleep. Ideas that had been accepted for centuries were swept away.

It was electronics that provided the tools with which

sleep and dreaming could be explored. Devices like the electroencephalograph to measure brain waves and muscle monitors which could detect the slightest tensing and relaxing of muscles showed that neither the body nor the mind were really at rest during sleep.

Today sleep is no longer regarded as a period of unconsciousness, broken only by an occasional dream. There is a regular rhythm to sleep. Each night every one of us goes through several stages of sleep, each quite different from the others. Indeed, some researchers believe that the word sleep is now obsolete because there are many different kinds of sleep.

The second startling discovery that came out of sleep laboratories concerned dreams. Dreams are not occasional events. They are regular nightly occurrences that appear to be absolutely essential to our physical and mental health. We all dream three or four times every night in about ninety-minute cycles.

. Scientists now believe that the mind is never entirely shut off during sleep, and that there is some kind of mental activity going on during even the deepest stages of sleep. Mental activity is simply more intense and vigorous during certain sleep periods. It is this more intense mental activity that we call dreaming. Indeed, the brain-wave pattern of a dreamer so closely resembles that of an awake person that some researchers prefer to call dream time paradoxical sleep.

Virtually all of the theorizing and speculation on the mystery and meaning of dreams that took place prior to the discovery of paradoxical sleep was based on second-hand reports. The only dreams that people had to work with were those that the sleeper happened to remember the next morning. The fact that some people were very poor at recalling dreams led to the idea that these people never dreamed or dreamed very rarely. But everybody dreams every night. Some people simply remember dreams better than others, but nobody, under normal circumstances, remembers all of their dreams every night.

Even those dreams that we do remember are often recalled in a garbled and incomplete manner. You have probably had the experience of waking up with vivid memories of a dream you just had. But within a very few minutes the details begin to slip away. By mid-morning you can hardly remember the dream at all.

Sleep laboratories have overcome some of these problems at least to a degree. With the proper monitoring equipment experimenters can tell with a fair degree of accuracy when a subject is dreaming. When the dream is over the subject can be awakened and recount his recollections into a tape recorder placed at bedside. His memory of a dream will be much fresher, and all the dreams of a night can be recalled, not just those in which the subject happened to wake up.

As a result of this research vast quantities of dream records have been collected in sleep laboratories throughout the world. Scientists have probably collected more authentic dream records in the last twenty years than had been collected in all the thousands of years that man has been trying to analyze and interpret his dreams.

But despite this vast record from research, the meaning of dreams is no clearer now than it was when the research first started. The collection of information, it seems, has merely deepened the confusion.

Worse yet, we don't even know what dreaming is for. If people or animals are deprived of dreams it can affect them mentally and physically. People who are drugged or mentally ill do not dream normally. Dreaming probably evolved early in mammalian history and has remained part of our heritage. Says Frederick Snyder of the National Institute of Mental Health, "the sheer universality, regularity, and lawfulness of the phenomenon smack of a basic biological process."

Dreaming is obviously good for something, but what? There is no lack of theories. But the evidence so far does not compel a belief in any one of them.

While modern sleep and dream research has provided no solid link between dreaming and creativity, the suggestion remains a probable one. One important element of creativity is the ability to break out of traditional or stereotypical ways of looking at a problem. Dreaming with its free-flowing and often fantastic imagery certainly provides this.

Dream research has also discovered that the majority of our dreams are involved with day-to-day concerns. If we are thinking about a problem during the day, we are very likely to dream about that very same problem at night.

We tend to think of dreams as being filled with bizarre and fantastical images. Some are, but many are not.

The same practical aspect was evident in a study of daydreaming conducted by psychologist Leonard M. Giambra. He studied 375 men between the ages of 17 and 90. Each was asked some three hundred questions about his daydreams.

Daydreaming is traditionally thought of as a period of

wish fulfillment. The classic story of the daydreamer is "The Secret Life of Walter Mitty" by James Thurber. Thurber's shy and ineffectual character constantly slips off into daydreams about heroic exploits. Real people do that sort of daydreaming, of course. This is particularly true when they are in their early twenties. But Giambra found that daydreaming for men of all ages was most commonly involved with problem solving. "Daydreams," the psychologist wrote, "are a flight from the immediate, but they often don't go far." Most daydreams, he found, concern the present and the future. Even the old men Giambra questioned spent relatively little time daydreaming about the past.

Giambra believes that daydreaming has a definite creative purpose. It serves, he says, as a sort of a mental back burner, in which information can be organized and reorganized creatively. "The fact that problem solving heads the lists of daydream types supports this interpretation."

Several studies have attempted to link nightly dreaming to personality type. As in other kinds of studies of personality type there is a certain ambiguity in the data. There is, for example, no firm agreement on what a "creative personality" is. The findings are interesting nonetheless.

Some studies found that people who were rated as artistically creative reported more vivid and imaginative dreams. This may be because the content of their dreams really is more vivid and imaginative or simply because they have a more colorful way of describing their dreams.

A good deal of attention has been devoted to the problem of how much sleep is necessary. Of course, since no one has been able to determine what sleep really does for us, it is impossible to know when we have had enough of it.

Enormous variations have been found in the amount of time people sleep. There are a few individuals who claim they do not sleep at all, or not more than a few minutes each night. Research seems to bear out such claims, though the cases are exceedingly rare. There are a fair number of people who sleep only three or four hours a night without any measurable ill effects. There also seems to be an equal number of perfectly normal people who need more than nine hours of sleep to function adequately.

One can find stories of highly creative people who claimed that they needed an exceptional amount of sleep, and stories of those who claimed that they practically never slept. Thomas Edison said that sleep was a waste of time. Modern research does not provide any clear choice between these contradictory sleep characteristics. In Boston, Ernest Hartmann compared the performance, health, and personalities of thirty short-sleepers and thirty long-sleepers. The short-sleepers were those who needed under five hours of sleep, the long sleepers those who regularly slept more than nine and a half hours. The short-sleepers seemed to be more efficient and well or ganized. The long-sleepers were more ethereal and sometimes downright disturbed. But they also tended to be engaged in more creative work.

Three studies of preschool children have indicated that the bright children slept somewhat less than their age-mates of average intelligence. On the other hand, Lewis Terman, a pioneer in psychological testing, conducted a massive study of gifted children and found that they slept more than their age-mates.

Despite the ocean of uncertainty that still exists about sleep and dreaming, there have been persistent and popular attempts in recent years to control dreaming and to use it more creatively. Several universities, particularly in California, now offer extremely popular courses on dream control. A book called *Creative Dreaming* by Dr. Patricia Garfield was a bestseller in California and had considerable success in other parts of the country. A growing number of psychologists and psychotherapists have turned from trying to analyze their patients' dreams to trying to get their patients to control their dreams and to use them creatively to solve problems of their waking hours.

The inspiration for the current creative dreaming enthusiasm does not come from laboratory studies. Rather it comes from the Senoi, a tribe of preliterate people who live in the rain forest of the Malay Peninsula.

The Senoi are one of those peoples who take their dreams very seriously. But the Senoi are not ruled by their dreams; rather, they try to control them and use them.

Each morning the Senoi family will gather to discuss the dreams of the previous night. If a Senoi child says that he has had a frightening dream of falling, his parents will congratulate him and tell him what a wonderful dream he has had. They explain that all dreams have a purpose. The next time he has such a dream he must relax with it and see where the fall takes him. Gradually a frightening dream of falling is converted into a joyous dream of flying.

The late Kilton Stewart, a research psychologist who

studied Senoi society for fifteen years, was enthusiastic about the results of the tribe's dream discussions. The Senoi have no war, no violent crime, and a high degree of mental health. "In the West the thinking we do while asleep usually remains on a muddled, childish, or psychotic level because we do not respond to dreams as socially important and include dreaming in the educative process," said Stewart.

There are responsible critics who claim that Stewart's assessment of the life of the Senoi is too idyllic. But no one disputes the fact that dreams dominate the Senoi world.

If a Senoi child dreams of having hurt someone, he goes to that person, apologizes, and offers a gift or favor. If he dreams that he was mistreated by someone he tells the guilty party, who attempts to compensate with a gift or friendly act. Thus conflicts are worked out through dreams.

After the breakfast discussion, the men of the tribe meet in councils to discuss their own dreams and to try to interpret more difficult ones. Dreams which seem to have a prophetic element are treated as important and authentic. Often a day's activities are planned around the dreams of the previous night.

Dr. Charles Tart, professor of psychology at the University of California at Davis, believes that the Senoi are able to work out many of their conflicts and problems in their dreams, and that all of us would benefit from their experience. "They [the Senoi] dream and then take an hour at breakfast time to discuss their dreams. Isn't mental health worth the price of an hour a day?"

Dr. Arnold Mysior of the Psychological Center of

Georgetown University uses some of the Senoi techniques in his own work. Once he even taught himself to fly—in his dreams of course.

> I just said to myself one evening, "Tonight in my dream I'm going to fly."
> Nothing. I didn't dream at all that night. The second night I said the same thing. Nothing.
> The third night it worked. There is probably an incubation period between the time you give yourself a suggestion and the time it takes effect. The funny thing about this particular dream was that I really didn't fly but I sort of scooted over the ground about three feet in the air, but with amazing speed. It was a marvelous dream.

Later Dr. Mysior saw a patient who had recurring nightmares about falling off a cliff. "Fly," he told her. And after a few nights of suggesting this to herself at bedtime, she did fly in her dreams, and that was the end of the nightmare.

Dr. Patricia Garfield believes that dreams can be used almost as rehearsals for real life situations. She says that like the Senoi we should train ourselves to confront our problems in our dreams and solve them. This is what is meant by creative dreaming.

But what if you are one of those who can't recall dreams? The solution is that you should take more interest in them. When psychoanalysis first became popular, patients spent a good deal of time discussing and interpreting dreams with their analysts. At first some patients said that they didn't dream very often, but as the analysis went on they reported dreaming more and more frequently. In fact, all they were doing was remembering their dreams more often as they became more interested in them.

Dream therapists suggest this technique for remembering your dreams more fully and accurately. Immediately upon awakening after a dream you may find that you do not remember the details very well. Perhaps all that you have is a vague awareness that you had been dreaming, or you may remember just snatches of the dream. You should then lie quietly and try to remember what you had been dreaming about. But don't try to force the memory or to provide new details that may make the dream more interesting. In most cases, if you relax the dream will come to you. On the other hand, don't relax too completely or you will go back to sleep. If the dream still slips away don't worry. There will be plenty of other opportunities.

If you wish to go into the creative dreaming techniques a bit more intensively, you can try waking yourself up several times a night to see if you can catch yourself in the middle of a dream. Since dreaming in the average person takes place approximately once every ninety minutes, you can set an alarm clock to go off about or a little more than an hour and a half after the time you think you will be asleep.

In a few nights you should be able to establish your own dreaming pattern. One problem with such a technique is that having your dreams interrupted night after night can cause psychological difficulties. In sleep studies some volunteers found themselves getting irritable after only a few nights of interrupted dreaming. If the experiments were carried on too long many volunteers became so upset that they quit the program. So be warned.

You should have pencil and pad by your bedside to write down your dreams. A tape recorder is even better. Some sort of permanent record will not only keep you from forgetting the dream altogether but will prevent you from unconsciously adding details that were not part of the dream itself.

There is the apocryphal story of the scientist who woke up with the solution to one of the most difficult problems in his field. But he didn't have any writing material handy. By the time he switched on the light and located pen and paper the solution had gone out of his head. There is no guarantee that you will wake up with any startling or original ideas. But in case you do, be prepared and don't let them slip away.

The physiologist Otto Loewi very nearly became the scientist in the story. In 1921 he was trying to find out whether any chemical phenomena were involved in nerve action. One night Loewi dreamed of an experiment which would test his theory. He wrote down his idea and went back to sleep. The next morning he was unable to read what he had written. Fortunately the next night he had the same dream. This time he went straight to his laboratory and performed the experiment.

Some people are able to teach themselves to wake up at the end of a dream, without any outside help, simply by willing it. Dr. Patricia Garfield, author of *Creative Dreaming*, has done this and verified her success by spending several nights in a laboratory with electric sensors near her eyes to measure rapid eye movements, an indication of dreaming.

Several times a night she wakes up and reaches for her pad and pen. She has even taught herself to write in the dark. She has learned to sense when the pen runs out of ink and uses her left hand as a marker at the beginning of each line to avoid overlapping her writing.

Over the years—since she was fourteen—she's amassed a huge collection of dream recalls. Her writings in the dark now comprise well over ten thousand dreams in seventeen volumes, more than filling a yard-wide bookcase. Here is a unique record of mental activity in a part of our life that is lost to most of us. Moreover, Dr. Garfield claims a growing degree of control over the practice of dreaming.

Will these popular dream control techniques help you control your life and make you a more fulfilled and creative person as their enthusiastic supporters claim? Or is this just one more in a long string of pop psychology fads? There is no solid research to support the values claimed for dream control. Perhaps the technique is too new to be adequately verified. Besides, attempts to measure such things as creativity and fulfillment have been notoriously unsuccessful.

But at the very least these techniques can help put you in touch with a part of your life once thought inaccessible and beyond control, and one which tradition has always linked with creativity.

8

Creativity and Brain Waves

Can anything be learned about creativity by studying the brain itself?

The hope that something can has been around for at least two centuries. How well it has been fulfilled to date is a subject that we will examine in this chapter.

In the nineteenth century scientists first began to make a solid philosophical connection between mind, that is, our thoughts and feelings, and brain, the approximately $2\frac{1}{2}$-pound grayish mass of interconnected nerve cells that sits within our skull.

The importance of the brain had, of course, been recognized long before the nineteenth century. But there had always been the suspicion that there was more to mind than brain, particularly for the "higher" mental activities of which creativity would certainly have been one. It was generally assumed that there were other subtle "spiritual forces" which affected the way an individual thought and acted. Creative people particularly were often regarded, and regarded themselves, as instruments for "inspiration" which came from beyond their physical brain. Some still do, even today.

The nineteenth century, however, witnessed the triumph of the physical sciences. This triumph was extremely significant in medicine, a subject which most closely affected man's view of himself. Ailments which had once been attributed to everything from sin to the influence of the planets were traced to changes within the physical body. A mass of theory developed which held that a person's intelligence, personality, and creative ability could be discerned by a study of his body and particularly of his brain.

The most exotic outgrowth from this perfectly reasonable line of thinking was phrenology. According to phrenology, various behavorial traits were centered in different and specific parts of the human brain. For example, if an individual had an exceptionally well-developed capacity for, let us say, love, the "love center" part of his brain would be larger than average. This would be reflected in a small difference in the shape of his skull, which fitted the brain like a glove and conformed to its contours. An expert phrenologist could determine the makeup of a person's brain by feeling his or her skull. In popular jargon, this was translated as feeling the "bumps" on your head.

Phrenology started out respectably enough, but it rapidly became a pseudoscience practiced by a host of uncritical enthusiasts or downright charlatans. Phrenologists still pop up occasionally at carnivals today, along with palmists, tea leaf readers, and other aging monuments to human gullibility. But it is important to remember that in the beginning there appeared to be some solid basis for phrenology. It is obvious foolishness today, but in the early 1800s its errors were not nearly so obvious. A good number of sincere and intelligent people believed in it and practiced it.

On a more sophisticated level, many scientists spent a great deal of time measuring people's skulls or weighing and measuring the brains taken from corpses. From these measurements they hoped to get some idea of what was going on in the mind.

Elaborate theories were developed about the shape and size of the brain and the number of wrinkles that it contained. None of these hypotheses proved to be much more productive than phrenology.

The fact is that the brain is far too complex an organ for anyone to be able to learn much about it by looking at it from the outside. One had to get inside the workings of the brain. But how? A partial answer to that question seemed to be provided in 1924.

In that year, an Austrian psychiatrist named Hans Berger tried an experiment with his fifteen-year-old son. He attached two pieces of silver foil to the boy's scalp, ran wires from them, and hooked the wires to a galvanometer (an instrument for measuring electrical current). Sure enough, there was an electrical current from the brain, weak but detectable.

For over a century it had been known that living bodies produced electrical energy, but this was the first time anyone had ever succeeded in measuring the electrical energy of the brain.

The electrical impulses that Berger measured later came to be called brain waves, the machine used to

*Phrenologists thought they could get a clue
to a person's mental process by studying
the shape of his skull.*

measure them the electroencephalograph. Berger continued his brain wave researches until 1938, when the Nazis deprived him of his university post.

Berger's early work was known but it did not attract immediate attention. In the late 1930s the prominent British psychologist Lord Adrian confirmed the main lines of Berger's work. Quite suddenly the psychological community became "brain wave conscious."

Some believed that the brain waves were the medium of telepathy; and they thought that sensitive individuals were able to pick up the electrical messages of one another's brains and interpret them, just as a radio receiver could pick up radio waves and convert them back into sound. Berger himself had entertained such ideas. More conventional researchers hoped that brain waves would at least provide insight into some forms of mental illness.

These high hopes were not fulfilled in the years to come. Brain waves did not prove to be nearly as useful as early researchers had hoped. Brain waves gave no real clues to what people were thinking. A study of electroencephalograms or EEGs did prove helpful in the diagnosis of epilepsy, brain tumors, or other severe brain injuries. But for normal brains Lord Adrian complained that EEGs were "disappointingly constant."

Yet in the 1970s brain waves have not only been the object of increased scientific attention, they have also become something of a cult, rivaling phrenology of a hundred and fifty years ago. Some contend that in brain waves can be found the key to the mystery of creativity and quite possibly to a method of increasing creativity.

Scientists have discovered four basic brain-wave patterns. Each has been given a letter of the Greek alphabet for identification purposes. The pattern with the highest frequency is called beta. Beta registers 13 cycles per second and above on the EEG. Next is alpha, which registers from approximately 8 to 13 cycles per second. Alpha is the first letter of the Greek alphabet, and the 8-to-13-cycle pattern was given that identification because it was discovered first. The brain generally registers alpha when a subject is sitting quietly with his eyes closed. Most early EEG subjects had the electrodes taped to their scalps and were then told to lie back, close their eyes, and relax. Naturally alpha showed up first. Besides, it is a well-defined pattern, one that is easy to identify, particularly with the primitive equipment that was all early brain-wave researchers had available. The faster beta waves are usually associated with a person who is awake and alert.

Theta waves are slower still, with a frequency of approximately 4 to 8 cycles per second. The slowest of all are delta waves from 1 to 4 cycles per second.

In any layman's discussion of brain waves, it is important to recognize that the subject is not nearly as simple as it can be made to sound. Like everything else about the brain, brain waves are both complex and controversial. For example, at any given time the entire brain does not "broadcast" just one type of brain wave. While electrodes placed on one part of the scalp may be picking up alpha, others may be picking up beta. Nor are the patterns always clear and identifiable. Very often they are jumbled together, with no clear pattern emerging.

Frequency is only one measure of brain waves. Amplitude is another. Amplitude is a measure of the strength of the electrical energy being picked up by the electrodes. It is displayed visually by the height of the peaks and depths of the valleys shown on the EEGs. At any frequency the amplitude may vary considerably. Just what these differences in amplitude may signify is far from clear. What is clear is that all alpha, beta, theta, or delta waves are not the same.

What is more difficult for the layman to appreciate about brain waves is that the EEG gives only the barest approximation of the brain's electrical activity. Though there is a great deal of electrical activity going on within the brain, the amount of voltage the brain puts out is tiny. It is measured in the one-hundred-millionths of a volt. Compare this to ordinary household electric current which is 120 volts. The EEG is only able to pick up those signals strong enough to penetrate the skull.

Trying to judge what goes on in the brain by EEG records alone is a bit like trying to find out what lives in the sea by examining only what floats to the surface. That tells us something, but the depths certainly hold many surprises. Still, EEGs are the only method available of keeping track of the human brain in action.

The EEG had a limited usefulness in neurology. It had generally been employed only to identify serious problems. When sleep and dream research began in earnest in the 1950s, the scientists used the EEG to keep track of the brain activity of their subjects. The EEG quickly revealed that the sleeping brain went through a variety of regular changes from beta to delta and back to near beta again several times during the night. This was the first time that extensive, prolonged EEG records had been taken from people with normal brains.

It had generally been assumed that brain waves were

quite beyond the conscious control of an individual. Then Joe Kamiya, a University of Chicago graduate student who had been one of the pioneers of sleep research, began to wonder whether a person knew when he was in one brain-wave state or another.

He decided to study alpha waves, because they seemed the easiest to produce and record. He told his volunteers that they were capable of producing a special brain-wave state that he called A—that was alpha. Anything else was called B. The subjects sat in a darkened room with electrodes taped to their heads. The wires led to an EEG machine which was out of their sight. When a bell rang they were supposed to guess as to whether they were in state A or B. At first they guessed right only about 50 percent of the time. That was pure chance.

But as the experiment went on and the subjects were told whether they were right or wrong, an unexpected development took place. After about an hour most subjects improved their accuracy to 60 percent. By three hours they were guessing right three times out of four. With further experience some subjects were able to guess state A correctly 100 percent of the time.

That a person could correctly identify a pattern of electrical activity from within his own brain seemed startling. But it was just a short step to an even more startling discovery. Once alpha could be identified, it could, to a great degree, be controlled.

During the early 1960s, the concept of biofeedback began to be extensively tested in laboratories. Biofeedback theory held that if an individual were made aware of certain internal biological activity, he might be able to consciously control that activity. This was true even if the activity was supposed to be beyond conscious control. Through training in biofeedback, people were able to exercise at least limited control over such "automatic" functions as blood pressure and heartbeat. It was control of brain waves that attracted most popular attention. With biofeedback, people could be trained to put themselves into the alpha state.

One of the major reasons why brain-wave-biofeedback training and particularly the alpha state has attracted so much public attention is that alpha became identified with meditation. Meditation, particularly as practiced by yogis from India and masters of Zen from Japan, had become increasingly popular in the West. Meditation seemed to hold out a promise of inner control and inner serenity that many in the West found irresistibly attractive.

When brain-wave readings of meditating yogis and Zen masters were taken, it was found that they were capable of producing sustained high amplitude alpha readings. They were able to hold the alpha state far longer than untrained individuals. Indeed, most of the meditative state seemed to be the alpha state, though theta waves might also appear as meditation deepened. High alpha production was also typical of those Westerners who had successfully completed the popular technique called Transcendental Meditation or TM. Alpha rapidly acquired some of the almost magical aura that had become attached to meditation itself.

The equipment needed for the initial alpha biofeedback experiments was cumbersome and expensive. Someone had to watch the tracings made on paper by the EEG machine and tell the subject when he was in alpha.

As the popularity of alpha biofeedback grew, simpler, more manageable equipment was produced. Today it is possible to purchase a small machine that hangs around your neck. You slip a headband containing electrodes around your head, put earphones over your ears, and listen for a tone signifying that the machine is picking up alpha waves from your brain. How well such machines really work is a matter of dispute, but they have been extremely popular. One Columbia University professor who had been involved in biofeedback experiments reported seeing a student walking along campus with one of these devices around his neck, listening for alpha.

The time in which the brain is registering predominantly alpha waves cannot definitely be linked with any particular mental or emotional state. But subjects of alpha biofeedback experiments most commonly indicated that when they were producing alpha they were in a state of "relaxed awareness." They were not asleep or not bored, but neither were they thinking about anything in particular. Many said that this state was highly pleasurable.

Normally one would not associate "relaxed awareness" with creativity. That would seem to require a far more active mental state. Yet some researchers have reported that creative people, artists, poets, and the like, were exceptionally good at producing alpha and easy subjects for alpha biofeedback training. Lester Fehmi, a biofeedback researcher at the State University of New York at Stony Brook, said that musicians, athletes, and artists were better than average subjects at alpha control.

Joe Kamiya told reporter Maya Pines of a poet who reported that his creative moments felt like the moments during which he was registering high alpha. This, reporter Pines pointed out, seemed rather strange, since one of the primary characteristics of the alpha state is that the subject does not have his attention focused on anything. The moment that attention becomes fixed, the subject slips out of alpha and into beta.

Kamiya replied: "That's one of the most peculiar things about it. It's probably best described as a shift in the focus of attention. You can't let yourself get drowsy, as this would take you out of alpha. You remain alert, expanding your focus of attention in all directions."

During alpha, the mind wanders. Perhaps it is then that the dissimilar elements of a problem can be linked up. Creativity has always been associated with freedom, and freedom of mind characterizes the alpha state. The best way to produce alpha say many who have tried it is by simply "letting go" mentally.

The experimental link between the alpha state and creativity was a fragile one. Yet the idea that high alpha production stimulated creativity became a basic tenet of the alpha cult. Perhaps the real reason for this identification was the feeling that alpha was good, creativity was good, and therefore these two good things must have something to do with each other.

Those involved in trying to control their own alpha production either through biofeedback or meditation would inevitably believe that they were "creative" people, in contrast to those rather stiff individuals who rejected the practice of alpha control or denounced it as foolishness. As we pointed out earlier, the word creative is all too often used as a synonym for "good" or "right."

A more interesting line of research was pursued at the

Menninger Foundation in Topeka, Kansas. There Drs. Elmer and Alyce Green had been doing a good deal of work with biofeedback. Alyce Green had also been involved in a research project on creativity. In studying the lives of famous artists, writers, and scientists she observed that many of them reported special mental states in which their minds were flooded with rich and unexpected images. Sometimes a creative solution to a problem might come out of such a mental state. These images could arrive during a dream, as in the case of Friedrich Kekulé. But the images could also come in the daytime during periods of quiet reverie or in daydreams.

The statements made by creative people seemed to Alyce Green very similar in nature to statements made by some of the brain-wave-biofeedback volunteers who were being trained to produce theta waves. Could there be some sort of a link between theta and creativity?

In order to probe this possible relationship more fully, the Greens started a project with twenty-six student volunteers from Washburn University in Topeka. These students were to be trained to increase production of both alpha and theta waves over a period of ten weeks.

During the first five weeks of the project the student volunteers learned how to increase the percentage of both alpha and theta waves when their eyes were closed.

Every other week the students came in for a training session. They were ushered into a dimly lit room and seated in comfortable reclining chairs. A headband containing electrodes was slipped on, and they then listened for the tones which signaled the production of alpha and theta. A low tone meant theta, a higher one alpha. In addition to the training sessions there were special rooms

Alyce Green: A link between theta waves and creativity?

set up at Washburn University for practice. Practice of at least an hour a day was required. The students also had to keep diaries of thoughts and feelings during this period.

During the second five weeks of the project the students were asked to concentrate on increasing their theta production. This proved to be much more difficult than producing alpha. But still most of the volunteers were able to increase theta production during the ten-week period of the project.

The Greens were especially interested in any strong spontaneous images that the subjects experienced while producing theta waves. These images might be pictures, sounds, touch, taste, smell, or any combination. Training sessions were occasionally interrupted by researchers who would ask "What's happening?" The subjects would then describe what they had just been experiencing.

Most of the volunteers seemed to enjoy the project. They reported that after training sessions they were more relaxed, calmer, and able to work better. Some said they felt "put together"—that their thoughts and memories sorted themselves out with less effort.

There were also reports of rather startling imagery during the feedback sessions. The images were often more akin to those reported by religious mystics than artists. For example, one subject saw an office in which he was looking frantically for information. Someone he had never seen before stepped out from behind a file cabinet and handed him a book saying, "The answer to everything you want to know is right in here." According to the subject the book contained Greek words and some pictures. "When I looked at the words," he said, "I knew, 'That is the truth.' That's what I was after."

It would be encouraging to report that theta training allowed people to go out and write beautiful poems or paint great pictures or make important scientific discoveries. None of this, however, can be said. There have been subjective reports from people who say that the training has allowed them to be more creative. But such reports are necessarily suspect. A person who believes that he is going to benefit from a particular course of action—in this case brain-wave biofeedback—is likely to report that he has indeed benefited. (In medicine that is called the placebo effect. A person is told that a particular pill will make him feel better. Then he is given a sugar pill which has absolutely no therapeutic effect whatsoever. Still the patient reports feeling better.)

The relationship between the theta state and vivid imagery, which crops up so frequently in any discussion of creativity, remains intriguing. It is an area that will undoubtedly be explored more fully in the years to come.

Psychologist Colin Martindale of the University of Maine has been studying the problems of creativity for years. Along with his associates he conducted a series of studies and experiments involving creativity and brain waves. His results often were quite contrary to the findings and claims of the alpha enthusiasts, but they have received much less popular attention.

Martindale had been intrigued by accounts of artists' extreme "sensitivity." In the folklore of artistic creation the artist must shut himself away from the outside world in order to "create." Once he was suitably isolated, the new ideas would come to him, not as the result of conscious calculation but fully developed from some unknown corner of the mind.

Were such tales true? Was it possible there was a physiological basis for them? Did the brains of highly creative people work differently than the brains of less creative people?

The best available method of answering these questions, Martindale felt, was to measure alpha waves. It wasn't alpha itself that he was interested in. Alpha was merely to be used as a measure of brain activity or more specifically activity within the cortex of the brain. Cortical arousal is the technical term. Cortical arousal increases as a person goes from sleep, to reverie and daydreams, to alert concentration, and finally to fear and panic.

In the waking brain the production of alpha is negatively related to cortical arousal; the more aroused his brain the fewer alpha waves a person produces. Normally we do our best rational work at medium levels of cortical arousal. If arousal is not high enough the mind drifts away from the task at hand; if too high then we are too upset and stressed to concentrate.

In order to divide highly creative from less creative subjects Martindale used two tests. One was the Alternate Uses Test ("How many uses can you think of for a brick?"). This is considered a test of "pure creativity."

The second test was the Remote Associations Test. The subject is given thirty sets of three words and asked to come up with a fourth word that is associated with the other three. For example, if one is given the words "cookie, sixteen, and heart," the associative word is "sweet." This test is considered to be a measure of intelligence and creativity.

The theory that Martindale wished to test was that creative people and uncreative people had different levels of cortical arousal under different conditions. In the first of the series of tests the alpha rhythms of the two groups were measured while resting. It was found that creative people produced less alpha than less creative people—even while resting, the brains of creative people were more active. Other physiological measurements also indicated that creative people were not as relaxed as the less creative.

This finding was followed up by three further experiments to test the sensitivity of creative people. When a loud high-pitched sound was played, the brain-wave patterns of creative people were more disrupted for a longer period than those of the less creative.

Volunteers were given an electric shock and asked to rate its intensity. Creative people consistently rated the shock as more intense than did the less creative. "The princess who felt the pea through 13 mattresses must have been extraordinarily innovative," commented Martindale.

Blindfolded subjects were asked to judge the size of a block of wood by running their fingers over it. The creative subjects regularly overestimated the size of the wood.

The conclusion of these experiments was that creative people who lock themselves away from distractions are not just being quirky. They really are bothered more severely by distractions than other people are. Under normal conditions, they simply have a higher level of cortical arousal.

But when brain waves were measured while subjects were taking the Alternate Uses creativity test, the opposite results showed up. Then it was the creative people who were operating at a high level of alpha, meaning low cortical arousal. The amount of alpha in the EEGs of the creative group went down for the Remote Associations Test, which is creativity plus intelligence, and down further still on a pure intelligence test. Yet on all of these tests the creative subjects showed a higher level of alpha than the less creative. For the uncreative, the amount of alpha dropped when they had to be creative. Says Martindale, "They [the less creative] concentrate too well and too earnestly; they focus on the trees and overlook the forest."

In another test, a group of students containing both creative and uncreative subjects was asked to make up a story. A similar mixed group was also asked to make up a story but told to make it as original as possible. This put them under some pressure to be creative.

The uncreative students produced the same amount of alpha whether trying to be creative or not. The creative students produced significantly more alpha when told to be original.

Early reports had indicated that creative people were better at learning to increase their alpha, so Martindale and his colleagues tested that proposition too. At first the creatives did learn alpha feedback more quickly. But the uncreatives soon caught up and passed them. In the long run, the creative people were less effective in learning to control their alph brain waves than were the uncreative people. Says Martindale, "Mind control and creativity, then, may be inversely related—if you're good at one you're probably not so good at the other."

Martindale cites the work of another psychologist, Gary Schwartz of Harvard, who gave creativity tests to teachers of Transcendental Meditation (TM). On some tests the meditators scored higher than the control groups, but on others they did no better or actually got lower scores than nonmeditators. "The results were especially interesting because the meditators were trying hard to succeed," said Schwartz.

While meditation and alpha biofeedback and a host of other "mind control" techniques have been touted as aids in increasing creativity, Martindale disagrees.

> It's possible, then, that all the effort to promote biofeedback gadgets, alpha machines and meditation, transcendental or otherwise, may have the side effect of decreasing our ability to think creatively. At least, if biofeedback doesn't actually decrease creativity, we can say that people who excel at it are not all that creative in the first place.

Such conclusions are hotly disputed by practitioners of alpha biofeedback and meditation, most of whom are passionately attached to these practices. In this area, as in all other areas of research involving the human brain, uncertainty and contradiction reign.

Martindale supports his thesis with the observation that one of the hallmarks of creativity is its spontaneous, uncontrolled nature, and that those who are able to control alpha would probably not be the most spontaneous and uncontrolled of people.

Martindale is convinced that the key to creativity is physiological. "We do not know yet whether imaginative people are made or born that way. . . . For the present, we can conclude that creative people view the world and react to it unlike most of their peers, not because they are eccentric and strange, but because they process information differently."

9

Two Brains

We talk about the human brain, but it would be more accurate to talk about the human brains. Inside our skulls is not one brain but two. Information about man's two brains has been coming out of laboratory and field studies over the last few years. This information indicates that our two brains have startlingly different functions. Some of these findings throw important new light on the problems of creativity. Indeed they may change our entire view of human consciousness.

If you look at a picture or model of the human brain you will see that it is split into two halves or hemispheres. These two hemispheres are connected by a thick bundle of nerves called the corpus callosum. The brains of other mammals also possess the same basic two-hemisphere makeup.

The physical structure of the brain has been known for centuries. It was also well known that each half of the brain exercised control over the opposite half of the body. An injury to the left half of the brain would affect the control of the right half of the body. The nerves that carry impulses from the body to the brain and vice versa cross over into the opposite side of the brain. Until roughly thirty years ago most scientists believed that the two halves of the brain were essentially mirror images of each other.

Then what function did the corpus callosum serve? No one really knew. In the laboratory the corpus callosum of animals was surgically cut to see what change in behavior the procedure produced. As far as observers could tell there was none. In the 1930s brain surgeons cut the corpus callosum of a patient in order to remove a deep brain tumor. They did not know what sort of personality changes such an apparently drastic operation might produce. They found no observable change.

Still it seemed highly unlikely that this large bundle of nerve fibers served no function at all, so experiments continued. Dr. Roger Sperry of the California Institute of Technology is generally recognized as the modern founder of split-brain research. Sperry suspected that the two halves of the brain were something more than mirror images.

Not only did injuries in one half of the brain affect muscular movements of the opposite half of the body, but, Sperry noted, there were also some less obvious effects. Patients who had injuries to the left half of their brains were more likely to lose the ability to speak than those who had right hemisphere injuries. Those who had right hemisphere injuries might find their spatial relations affected, whereas those with left hemisphere injuries would not.

As early as 1864, the eminent neurologist John Hugh-

lings Jackson had published observations on the differences in function between the two hemispheres of the
brain. He described the left hemisphere as the seat of the
"faculty of expression." He also said that a patient with a
tumor in the right hemisphere did not know objects,
persons, and places. Jackson was not the only one to make
such observations. But these findings were generally
overlooked because no one knew quite what to do with
them.

Sperry began his investigation of the two halves of the
brain with animals. One of his graduate students conducted a series of experiments with split-brain cats—that
is, cats which have had the two halves of the brain surgically separated. The student, Ronald Myers, found that
split-brain cats that had been trained to recognize a pattern with one eye covered were completely unable to
recognize it with the other eye. Thus it was proved con-
clusively that the corpus callosum transferred memory
from one side of the brain to the other. If it was cut, the
animals behaved as if they had two entirely separate
brains that did not communicate with one another.

Experiments have shown that the functions in animals
of the two halves of the brain appear to be roughly the
same, at least as far as we can tell. In human beings this is
not the case. Language, we know, is centered in the left
hemisphere. Animals who do not possess a high degree of
language cannot be tested for this. In order to discover
what other differences there may be between the two
halves of the human brain, tests must be conducted on
human beings. Therefore progress in this area has been
understandably slow. Brain surgery in which the corpus
callosum is cut is very rare. Often the patients upon

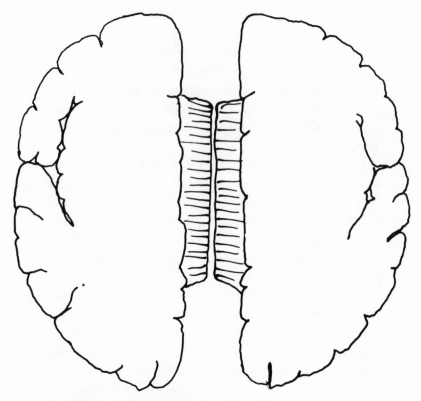

The human brain is divided into two halves
or hemispheres. The right half of the brain controls
the left half of the body, and vice versa.

whom such surgery has been performed are so gravely ill that they are unable or unwilling to participate in further psychological studies.

In 1961 Dr. Sperry found a cooperative and exceedingly interesting subject. He called the man W. J. W. J. had received severe head injuries during World War II. A few years later he began to suffer from epileptic seizures. Nothing seemed to relieve the seizures, which were becoming worse and worse. Finally in desperation surgeons severed his corpus callosum. The seizures stopped immediately, but for over a month W. J. was unable to speak. When he did recover his speech he said he felt much better. Surgeons at first feared that the operation might produce some sort of massive personality changes in the patient. But these fears did not appear to be justified.

W. J. agreed to undergo a series of tests, and the task was taken up by Michael Gazzaniga, another one of Sperry's graduate students. It soon became apparent that W. J. was very far from what we would call "normal." He was a person for whom the old saying about the right hand not knowing what the left was doing applied very literally.

W. J.'s left hand, controlled by the right hemisphere of his brain, not only didn't know what the right was doing, it seemed unable to understand spoken instructions. And it was aggressive and unreliable to boot. The result was like something out of a science fiction story. At one point W. J. attempted to strike his wife with his left hand, while his right hand tried to stop it.

Once Gazzaniga and W. J. were playing horseshoes in W. J.'s back yard. The student saw W. J. pick up an ax with his antisocial left hand and decided to leave the scene immediately. He later told reporter Maya Pines, "It was entirely likely that the more aggressive right hemisphere might be in control." Gazzaniga knew that he couldn't reason with the right hemisphere because it didn't understand language. He feared that he might become part of a test case: "Which half-brain does society punish or execute?"

A variety of tests indicated that the left half of W. J.'s brain was far more useful than the right half. Researchers began to wonder what the right half of the brain was needed for in the first place. But what underlay the apparent uselessness of the right half of the brain was that all language faculties were in the left half. The right half of his brain might be doing a great deal but it couldn't tell anyone.

When presented with a printed page, W. J. could only read those words in the right half of his visual field—that is, the half controlled by the left hemisphere of his brain. He could see perfectly well with his left eye, but when the visual images were carried to the right half of his brain it lacked the ability to interpret these images. Without the corpus callosum's connecting the two halves of the brain the right brain was cut off from those portions of the brain which interpret language.

A great deal of modern life depends on language. Certainly a great deal of psychological testing does. That is why the right half of W. J.'s brain seemed so useless. But it wasn't. In one test W. J. was asked to copy a picture of a Greek cross. Though he was right-handed, he was able to draw the cross smoothly and accurately with his left hand. But his right hand failed at the task. Yet he wrote perfectly well with his right hand and could not with his left. Before the operation, he had been able to write a few words with his left hand. Most right-handed people can. What underlay the difference was not muscular control of the hand but language.

Over the years Sperry has tested nearly twenty split-brain patients in his laboratory. They did not all react in exactly the same manner. W. J. still showed the most dramatic split-brain behavior, but he had also sustained considerable brain damage beyond the severing of the corpus callosum. Even in a split-brain patient, the right hemisphere can still control some movements of the right hand as well as of the left. Yet the results of many of these tests provide striking demonstrations of how the two brains in our skull operate.

Two of Sperry's associates, Drs. Colwyn Trevarthen and Jerre Levy, devised a facial recognition test. They took pictures of faces, cut them in half, and then rearranged them in different combinations. They deliberately produced strange combinations; for example, half of the face of a young black man would be matched up with half of the face of an elderly white woman. These combined pictures were then projected on a screen in front of split-brain subjects. The subject was told to keep his eyes focused on a red dot in the middle of the picture. The aim was to have one-half of the picture in the field of vision of the left eye, controlled by the right brain, and the other half of the picture in the field of vision of the right eye, controlled by the left brain.

After the composite picture was flashed briefly on a screen the subject was shown several pictures and asked to point to the face he had seen. Invariably the split-brain patient pointed to the picture whose half-face had been projected in front of his left eye. It seemed clear to researchers that the right brain was dominant in this type of recognition.

But when the patient was asked to *tell* which picture he had seen he usually chose the picture that had appeared before his right eye, that is, the eye controlled by the language-oriented left brain. But the choice in this case was more tentative. Often the patient seemed confused and unable to remember which face he had seen.

The conclusion drawn from such tests was that the right brain is better at recognizing a total picture or scene. However, without the aid of the left brain it cannot express what it recognizes except with a gesture. When speech is called for the left brain takes over, but it is not nearly so competent in the task of recognition.

In one experiment Sperry was showing a series of slides to a split-brain subject. The photos were dull, but at one point a picture of a nude woman was exposed to the left eye, thus the right hemisphere of the patient. The patient, a woman, said she saw nothing, but she blushed and became very uncomfortable. When the nude was flashed in her left visual field again, she still insisted that she had seen nothing, but her embarrassment became even more obvious. The verbal left half of her brain didn't know what was going on. The right half of her brain had triggered an emotional reaction. Finally she told Sperry that he had a very funny machine.

Research indicates that the great differences in function of the two brain halves are not inborn but develop as a human being grows. Young children who have had serious brain injuries seem to be able to compensate for the injury far more easily than an adult can. If a child under the age of five or even ten has had a large portion of the left hemisphere of his brain destroyed he will still be able to learn to speak again. If a child has an injury to the right brain he will still experience some difficulty in speaking. Language has not yet been centered in one hemisphere of the brain. In adults the center of language appears to be firmly fixed in the left brain. An adult who loses his speech due to an injury of the left brain will not be able to learn to speak again. But speech will be unaffected if the injury is confined to the right brain.

Dr. Sperry believes that the two hemispheres of the brain potentially compete with each other for dominance and that "excellence in one tends to interfere with top-level performance in the other." Thus one side of the brain inevitably comes to dominate the other. Since so much of modern life depends upon language, it is generally the left side that dominates.

If Roger Sperry is the father of two-brain research, then its chief apostle and most effective spokesman is a young California psychologist named Robert E. Ornstein. Ornstein has been able to command a degree of media attention that is rare for a scientist. In 1973 the *New Yorker* magazine even sent a special correspondent to California to report on the psychologist's lavish 32nd birthday party. During the party Ornstein was presented with a cake which read "Happy Hemispherical Birthday."

While many experimental psychologists who have worked in split-brain research are cautious, even timid,

*Psychologist Robert Ornstein, the leading apostle
of right and left thinking.*

about drawing sweeping conclusions (at least in public),
Ornstein is not. Writing in the magazine *Psychology Today*, Ornstein says,

> The belief there are two forms of consciousness has been
> with us for centuries. Reason versus passion is one of its
> guises, mind versus intuition is another. The feminine, the
> sacred, the mysterious historically have lined up against
> the masculine, the profane and the logical. Medicine ar-
> gues with art, yin complements yang. In fable and folk-
> lore, religion and science, this dualism has recurred with
> stunning regularity.
>
> What is new is the discovery that the two modes of
> consciousness have a physiological basis. They are not
> simply a reflection of culture or philosophy. The evidence
> accumulated that the human brain has specialized and that
> each half of that organ is responsible for a distinct mode of
> thought.

Sigmund Freud, the founder of psychoanalysis, pos-
tulated a conscious and an unconscious mind. He held
that the conscious mind largely controlled language and
other rational activities, and the unconscious mind was
less accessible to reason and verbal analysis.

The Freudian dichotomy was extremely influential.
Not only did it shape psychoanalytic theory, it has also
become part of the way in which we all regard the human
personality. When we do something that is unexpected
and that we did not rationally decide upon, we may say
that we acted from an "unconscious" or "subconscious"
drive or need.

The idea of the unconscious has also affected the way
we think about creativity and the creative person. Some

theorists have said that the unconscious is a vast storehouse from which many creative impulses or inspirations rise unexpectedly to the conscious mind.

One of the major criticisms of the theory of the unconscious mind was that it seemed rather mystical. Where, critics asked, was the unconscious located? Ornstein is able to see at least a "loose analogy" between the verbal left brain and the conscious, and the silent but still very active right brain and the Freudian unconscious.

Over the last few years Ornstein and his colleague David Galin at the Langley Porter Neuropsychiatric Institute of the University of California have begun to carry on research on the two halves of the brains of normal people with the aid of EEGs.

These tests indicate that the division of labor in the two halves of the normal brain are about the same as they are in the split-brain individuals. The right brain is good at some tasks, the left brain at others. In a test of fifty normal people, Ornstein found that their left brains remained comparatively idle, showing slow waves including alpha, while they arranged colored blocks and designs. EEGs from the right side of the brain, however, revealed the faster waves of activity and attention.

When the same subjects switched to a verbal activity like letter writing, the activity of the brain picked up on the left side and died down on the right. The same pattern was observed when the subjects were asked just to think about writing a letter.

Other tasks which stimulated the left brain were reading a column of print, doing arithmetic, and making up a list of words beginning with a particular letter. But when the volunteers were asked to remember a musical tone or draw a simple design it was the right side of the brain that became active once again.

Ideally the two halves of the brain should cooperate, with each taking up whatever task it is best suited for. In fact, Ornstein believes that the two halves of the brain do not completely balance each other in the average person. "Most people are dominated by one mode or the other," he wrote in *Psychology Today.* "They either have difficulty in dealing with crafts and body movements, or difficulty with language."

The dominance of one half of the brain over the other is probably cultural rather than hereditary, Ornstein believes. Western society in general tends to put more stress on the rational and the verbal—it is a left-headed society. But in some areas right-headedness predominates. Children in poor black neighborhoods, for example, learn to use their right hemispheres. Under such conditions they grow up being better at sports and music, poorer at verbal tasks. The left-headed person has trouble with physical movements, because his left hemisphere tends to analyze the movements, and that slows them down.

O. J. Simpson, a great athlete, says that he does his best running when he doesn't analyze. He just acts "instinctively."

It is really quite impossible to learn activities that involve physical movement from a book. Have you ever tried to learn sleight-of-hand magic from an instruction manual? You can't do it. Though you know how the trick is done, you still can't pull it off adequately. The same is true of skiing, tennis, or bike riding. You can't learn them from a book or from verbal instructions alone. You have to practice, and usually someone has to show you how to do it. The left brain may understand the instructions perfectly well, but it is the right brain which controls the activity, and words mean nothing to the right brain.

"The two modes of thought complement each other, but one does not readily replace the other," says Ornstein. "Try to describe a spiral staircase without using your hands."

There are a couple of simple right- and left-brain tests that you can try yourself. Marcel Kinsbourne of Duke University devised this one. Ask a friend to balance an ordinary wooden dowel on the index finger of each hand. Usually right-handed people do better with the right hand and left-handed people with the left.

Now ask your friend to speak while balancing the dowel, and measure the time that he or she is able to keep the dowel balanced. Kinsbourne found that the balancing time of right-handed people using their right hand fell off. Talking placed an extra burden on the left brain. But the balancing time of the left hand increased.

Dr. Ernest Hilgard of Stanford University asks people to count the letters in the word Minnesota. Then he looks into their eyes, to see which way they shift—if to the right that means the left part of their brain is more easily activated than the right.

Ornstein believes the kind of question affects the way you shift your gaze. If the question is verbal, the eyes will shift to the right. If it is spatial, such as "Which way does George Washington face on a quarter?" more eyes will shift to the left.

If there are two distinct modes of thought, is it possible that there are two distinct types of creativity, one centered in the left brain, the other in the right? Ornstein tested a group of lawyers, members of a profession he considers to be definitely left-brained, and a like number of sculptors and ceramic artists, right-brained people. The EEGs from the two groups showed that the lawyers have more active left brains whereas the sculptors and ceramic artists have more active right brains.

Historically, Western society has favored the left-brained, rational approach. Intellectuals have often scorned as "stupid" the visual artist and the athlete who could not be verbally articulate. Artists and athletes have often responded with equal scorn, regarding the talky intellectuals as out of touch with what is real and important. In fact, the brains of both of these groups may simply operate in different ways, without one's being necessarily superior to the other.

Recently right-brained activities have been enjoying something of a renaissance in the West. There has been increased interest in Oriental religion—a mode of thinking that Ornstein considers distinctly right-brained. You can't describe nirvana. The popular "human potential" movement, which stresses such things as "sensitivity training" and "body awareness," is also distinctly right-brained. The whole counterculture of the sixties was, in the view of many, a right-brained movement, for it stressed "feeling" over "thought."

California's Esalen Institute, the breeding place of many of the currently popular sensory awareness techniques, has been described as a right-brained citadel. Says Adam Smith, the pseudonymous chronicler of pop cultural fads, "Esalen was the counter-culture's university, where the right-brained techniques could surface, and the right-brained ideas could find articulation." In his book *The Mind Field*, Robert Ornstein states:

> Most of us have been educated and have developed sequential abilities (readin', 'ritin', and 'rithmetic) at the expense of the fluid and simultaneous. Many well-trained verbally say they cannot "understand" art, the rationalist opposes the "mystic," partly because we attribute only our verbal-analytic abilities to our "mind" while often denying "mental" status to the intuitive. We may compliment a painter or photographer's "eye," a craftsman's "touch," an artist for an apt "gut" feeling—and rarely for the powers of their mind.

We value the verbal, left-brained side of the mental function so highly that often when we say that someone has a great mind we may mean only that he has a great mouth.

The right-brained/left-brained dichotomy may throw some light on the phenomenon of "enlightenment" or "illumination." Frequently, people creative and otherwise report being suddenly overwhelmed by an experience or feeling that they are unable to describe. Sometimes this experience is defined as being religious or mystical. Often it can change a person's entire outlook on life. Usually such experiences come during a period of prolonged meditation or prayer or in the aftermath of a personal crisis—the death of a loved one, perhaps.

Many psychologists now believe that this experience is the result of the temporary dominance of the right half of the brain over the left. Just why the sudden switch in dominance should take place at all is unknown. But psychologists now do believe that they are beginning to understand the physiological mechanism behind the mystic experience.

The discovery of the differences between the right and left hemispheres of the brain throws important light on the subject of creativity. There can be, it seems, two distinctly different types of creative people. Today, consumer advocate Ralph Nader is often cited as the perfect left-brained type. He is brilliantly logical and extremely articulate, but he has no interests outside his work and is in no way considered to be artistic. And he can't dance.

But the division between right- and left-brained types of creativity is not always simple, for not all creative people can be divided neatly into one of the two camps. Take the case of Albert Einstein. Mathematics is a left-brained activity. Einstein was also an unusually good writer. He might seem a perfect example of the left-brained type—but he wasn't.

Einstein loved music and was an excellent violinist—music is right-brained. More significantly, Einstein reported that most of his important ideas did not come to him in words but in images.

"A thought comes, and I may try to express it in words afterwards," he wrote. He described some of his most creative thoughts as "physical entities"—certain kinds of signs and images. Some of these signs were "of visual and some of muscular type. Conventional words or other signs have to be sought for laboriously only in a secondary stage, when the mentioned associative play is sufficiently established and can be reproduced at will."

So the nonverbal, nonintellectual right side of the brain may well have contributed greatly to the creative activity of the man who is perhaps the primary symbol of intelligence in the twentieth century. "The really valuable thing," said Einstein, "is intuition." Intuition may arise from the right half of the brain.

One cannot describe or explain intuition. If it is a right-brain activity this is hardly surprising, for the right brain is not the center for language; it is not verbal. Yet many of us tend to believe that what cannot be explained or described either doesn't exist or isn't very important. We tend to regard knowledge arrived at in an intuitive, nonverbal way as inferior and not really knowledge at all. That attitude will have to change. Just because the right brain cannot speak does not mean it is unimportant. Scientists as well as artists need intuition.

For many creative endeavors, intuition which may be due to the action of the right brain is only the first step in the process. Ornstein, who has done so much to popularize the use of the right brain, is quite clear about this. In his book *The Psychology of Consciousness* he writes:

> In the writing of this book, I have had vague idea after idea at different times: on the beach, in the mountains, in discussion, even while writing. These intuitions are sparse images—perhaps a connection which allows a new gestalt [a psychological term meaning, roughly, the whole picture] to form—but they are never fully clear, and never satisfactory by themselves. They are incomplete realizations, not a finished work. For me, it is only when the intellect has worked out these glimpses of form that the intuition becomes of any use to others. It is the very linearity of a book which enables the writer to refine his own intuitions, and clarify them, first to himself, and then if possible to the reader.

Most of us have had the experience of getting an idea—an intuition we might call it—then finding how difficult it is to express the idea in a meaningful or practical way. Perhaps it is lack of coordination between our nonverbal right hemisphere, where the idea originates, and our verbal and logical left hemisphere, which should be able to work the idea out.

Research on the differences between the right and left hemispheres of the human brain has not led to any final answers about human creativity. Many psychologists would dispute the importance that men like Robert Ornstein places upon the hemispheres. Still there is no dispute that the research has turned up some fascinating possibilities. The left brain, it seems, has been able to unlock some of the secrets of the right brain.

It is tempting to conclude that with our new scientific instruments and growing knowledge of brain physiology the problems associated with creativity will soon be solved. Tempting but probably not true for several reasons.

First, as we said at the very beginning of this book, creativity is not a scientifically precise word. What we call creativity almost certainly involves a large number of different mental functions, which operate in highly individualized ways in different people.

More basically we must admit that while we have learned a good deal about brain function over the last century, the brain still remains largely unexplored territory. Scientists who have worked in brain research marvel at the complexitiy of the organ and are humbled by how little they really know about it. These scientists do not expect any quick and dramatic breakthroughs but rather a slow accumulation of research information. So much of the "mystery" of creativity is going to remain with us for a long time to come.

But some useful things have been learned, and we can summarize them briefly.

Creativity is a function of the brain, and its beginnings can probably be traced in our evolutionary heritage.

Highly creative people are rarely mad and may in fact enjoy better mental and physical health than the general run of the population.

The highly creative, however, either are or are allowed to be somewhat more adventurous and eccentric.

High creativity and high intelligence are not necessarily the same.

Some degree of creativity seems to be present in all of us.

Creativity cannot flourish in a vacuum. Social conditions must allow, and preferably encourage, creative activity.

That most mysterious element of creativity, intuition or inspiration, may arise in the right hemisphere of our brain.

This is admittedly not a great deal of hard information on a subject that has been studied and pondered for so long by so many. But it is a start.

Selected Bibliography

Barron, Frank. *The Creative Person*. Berkeley: University of California Press, 1961.

Berelson, Bernard, and Steiner, Gary A., eds. *Human Behavior*. New York: Harcourt, Brace and World, 1964.

Cohen, Daniel. *Intelligence: What Is It?* New York: Evans, 1974.

Dubois, René and Jean. *The White Plague: Tuberculosis, Man and Society*. London: Victor Gollancz, 1953.

Ferguson, Marilyn. *The Brain Revolution*. New York: Taplinger, 1973.

Getzels, Jacob, and Jackson, Philip. *Creativity and Intelligence: Explorations with Gifted Students*. New York: Wiley, 1962.

Ghiselin, Brewster. *The Creative Process*. Berkeley: University of California Press, 1952.

Giambra, Leonard M. "Daydreams." *Psychology Today*, July 1976.

Hatterer, Lawrence J. *The Artist in Society*. New York: Grove Press, 1965.

Koestler, Arthur. *The Act of Creation*. New York: Macmillan, 1964.

Luce, Gay Gaer. *Biological Rhythms in Human and Animal Physiology*. New York: Dover, 1971.

Martindale, Colin. "What Makes Creative People Different?" *Psychology Today*, July 1975.

May, Rollo. *The Courage to Create*. New York: Norton, 1975.

Mooney, Ross, and Razik, Taher, eds. *Explorations in Creativity*. New York: Harper and Row, 1967.

Morris, Desmond. *The Biology of Art*. London: Methuen, 1962.

——, and Morris, Ramona. *Men and Apes*. New York: McGraw-Hill, 1966.

Ornstein, Robert. *The Mind Field*. New York: Viking, 1976.

——, ed. *The Nature of Human Consciousness*. New York: The Viking Press, 1973.

——. *The Psychology of Consciousness*. New York: Viking, 1972.

——. "Right and Left Thinking." *Psychology Today*, May 1973.

Pickering, George. *Creative Malady*. New York: Oxford University Press, 1974.

Pines, Maya. *The Brain Changers*. New York: Harcourt, Brace, Jovanovich, 1973.

Rosner, Stanley, and Abt, Lawrence E., eds. *The Creative Experience*. New York: Grossman, 1970.

Schwartz, Gary E. "The Facts on Transcendental Meditation, Part II." *Psychology Today*, April 1974.

Smith, P., ed. *Creativity*. New York: Hastings House, 1959.

Watson, J. D. *The Double Helix*. New York: Atheneum, 1968.

Williams, Gurney. "How to Control Your Dreams." *Science Digest*, July 1976.

Index

Picture Credits